How to
SKETCH
ALWYN CRAWSHAW

HPBooks®

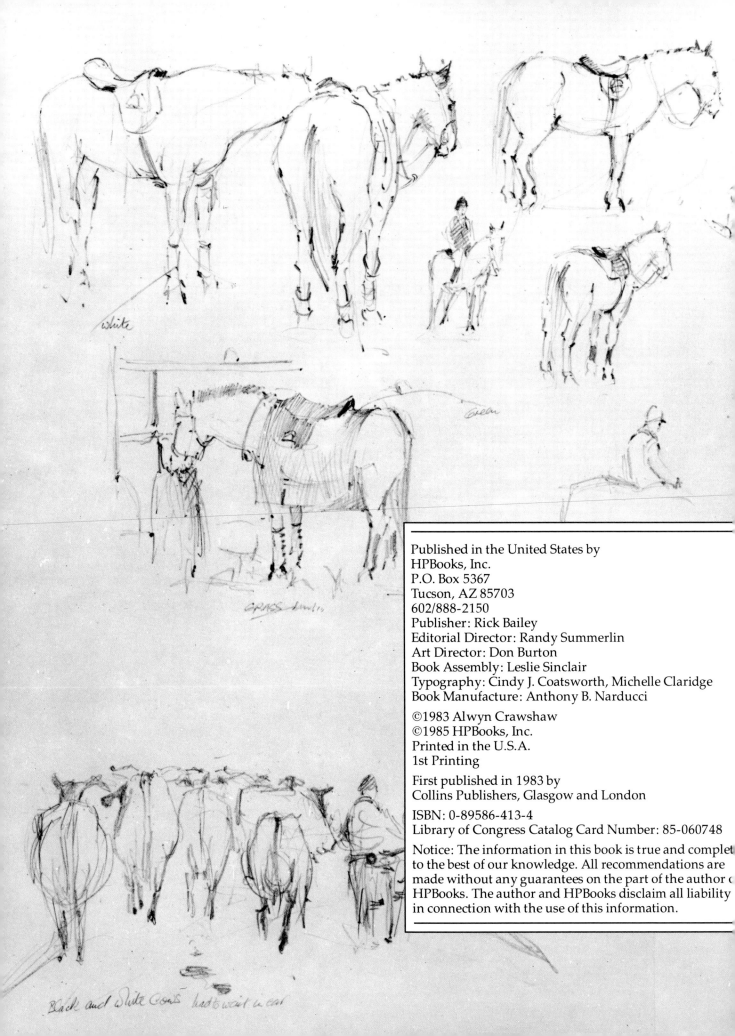

white

Grass

Grass Jan/

Published in the United States by
HPBooks, Inc.
P.O. Box 5367
Tucson, AZ 85703
602/888-2150
Publisher: Rick Bailey
Editorial Director: Randy Summerlin
Art Director: Don Burton
Book Assembly: Leslie Sinclair
Typography: Cindy J. Coatsworth, Michelle Claridge
Book Manufacture: Anthony B. Narducci

©1983 Alwyn Crawshaw
©1985 HPBooks, Inc.
Printed in the U.S.A.
1st Printing

First published in 1983 by
Collins Publishers, Glasgow and London

ISBN: 0-89586-413-4
Library of Congress Catalog Card Number: 85-060748

Black and White Cows had to wait u eat

CONTENTS

Artist's Sketch — Alwyn Crawshaw

Alwyn Crawshaw was born in 1934 at Mirfield, Yorkshire, England. He now lives in Devon. During his school years he studied at the Hastings School of Art, where he specialized in watercolors and oil painting. He now works in those and other media—including pastels, acrylics and the sketching media discussed in this book.

Crawshaw is a successful painter, author and lecturer. His work has brought him recognition as one of the leading authorities in his field. In addition to this book, he is the author of other books in the series, including *How to Paint Landscapes, How to Paint Boats & Harbors, How to Paint With Watercolors* and *How to Paint With Acrylics.*

Crawshaw is most interested in *realistic subjects,* such as landscapes and still lifes. This work has received much critical acclaim, starting with his painting *Wet and Windy.* It was one of the top 10 prints chosen by members of the Fine Art Trade Guild in 1975. His paintings are in art galleries and private collections throughout the world. His work has also been exhibited in group and one-man shows in England and several European countries. Admirers enjoy the reality and atmosphere conveyed in his work.

In addition to his frequent lectures and demonstrations to art societies, Crawshaw has discussed painting techniques on British radio and television.

Wind and Fire, 30x15 inches, watercolor. Author's collection.

Since moving to the country, Crawshaw sketches more than ever. All he has to do is walk out of his house with sketchbook and pencil and start working in the beautiful surrounding countryside. Because sketching is the basis of all drawing and painting, Crawshaw does it regularly. He recommends that you do the same because by sketching you can observe and learn. He finds that a sketching day frequently will turn into a family day with his wife and children. Or, as his wife, June, comments, a family day out will quickly turn into a sketching day!

According to Crawshaw, there are two attributes necessary for artistic success: *dedication* and *a sense of humor.* The need for the first is obvious. The second "helps you out of many a crisis." This book will help you with both.

Sidmouth, Devon, 10x7 inches, acrylic. Private collection.

Let's Sketch

A sketch is the beginning of artistic work. It's safe to say that practically everything that has been created on paper, canvas, clay, stone, metal, wood, or indeed any artist's medium, was first recorded as a sketch.

An idea can be stimulated by a thousand things, but a sketch can hold it for all time. It's used as a foundation for subsequent work, even though the idea may represent only a fleeting moment of inspiration. Sketching is a way to record something forever. For this reason I repeatedly stress the following throughout this book: *Never throw a sketch away, no matter how small or insignificant you think it is.* You have created something original that can help you now or years later.

If you accept my belief that the sketch is the beginning, then you can also see that sketching is a fine way to learn how to draw and paint finished pictures. In this book you will learn how to sketch just about anywhere and *use* your sketches—either as finished works or as training exercises for subsequent drawings and paintings. This way you can build on the knowledge you already have.

If you are a beginner, you will begin to really *see* new sights worth recording. Who knows? You might eventually look at a telephone pole and wonder at its beauty!

If you reach this stage, it may be wise to keep your feelings to yourself. This is not to say that artists are not normal people. They are. Rather, let your sketches and paintings reflect your wonderment. Focusing your feelings into your work will improve it and make it quite eloquent!

Along this line, it is interesting that we always think of ourselves as acting normal, no matter what profession, sport or pastime we enjoy. The following anecdote shows what I mean: On one occasion I went sketching to gather material for this book. My wife and I ended up at a cold, seaside river and estuary. The sea was very shallow in this area and covered with windsurfers skimming across the water. They were falling in, getting up, and falling in—over and over again. Although they had wetsuits on, they looked extremely cold. We thought they were silly.

Further along the stony beach we saw two bundles of clothing with what looked like a long antenna sticking out. When we were closer, a head popped up and said, "Good afternoon." They were fishermen somehow enjoying themselves on a bleak and frigid day. We acknowledged them and went on.

Eventually I found a suitable spot to put my chair down and started to sketch the scene in front of me. The wind was so sharp that I was only able to sketch for about 20 minutes. My wife, June, had gone for a walk to try to keep warm. When I had almost finished, one of the fishermen came over to me and looked at my right hand blue with cold, and my left hand with a glove on. He said, "You must be crazy sitting out here drawing a picture."

The funny part is that I thought I was the normal one; the anglers and windsurfers were the oddballs! So perhaps being odd is only in the eye of the beholder. The sketch I did on that occasion was drawn with a 2B pencil on heavyweight paper. It's pictured below.

I am not suggesting that you go out and find the coldest spot and stick it out for 20 minutes. What I want you to do after reading this book is go out with confidence and *enjoy* sketching, regardless of the circumstances. Incidentally, I enjoyed doing the

Venn Ottery Church, 7x10 inches.

sketch described, but I still can't understand how the windsurfers enjoyed their time!

I enjoy sketching as much as sitting in my studio painting a "masterpiece." One of the greatest advantages of sketching is that it gives a good reason to go out and enjoy your surroundings, even if it is only to your own backyard. For example, the photograph on page 6 shows me in my garden sketching two new additions to the family. The ducks were an

Exmouth—A Cold Day, 11x9 inches.

Twin Elms, Cambridge, 8-1/2x11 inches. In this information sketch, the trees are the main element. I indicated scale by including the sheep and figure.

Me In Bed, 11x8-1/2 inches. This is a typical enjoyment sketch.

anniversary present from our daughter and her husband. The resulting sketch is on page 23.

WHAT IS IN THIS BOOK

I have tried to write this book in a logical order, but because there is so much to say almost at the same time, it can be difficult. For instance, which comes first, the section on composition or notes on perspective, how to use a pencil or what types of sketch to do? To overcome this I suggest that you read the book all the way through—even though at times it may seem as though the cart is being put before the horse. Then you can go back to appropriate sections in whatever order suits you best.

Except for the exercises, all the sketches in the book are reproduced from my sketchbooks. All were done on location—some especially for the book, others from my work over the past few years. This should give a broad overview of sketching and a variety of subjects. In fact, each sketch tells *me* a story. I feel as though I am opening the pages of my private sketching life and sharing it with you. By doing this, I hope that you will learn from my experiences and have splendid ones of your own.

SOME DEFINITIONS

Now let's get back to the drawing board. We know that a sketch is the beginning, but what does the word really mean? Artists use it to mean a variety of things. For example, a *quick sketch* can mean something carefully observed and created with only a dozen lines, or a picture that hasn't made the grade in the artist's eyes. In this case, he might say disparagingly, "It's just a quick sketch."

One artist may use just a pencil and small pad when sketching. Another might take everything he can think of—easel, canvases, paints, seat, small table, umbrella, and more—to go sketching.

Because of the imprecise use of the word *sketch,* I have defined certain types of sketching. This is from the artist's point of view, so it will help you through this book. After much thought I have separated sketching into four main categories:

Enjoyment Sketch—A drawing or painting you do on location, done simply to enjoy the experience.
Information Sketch—A drawing or painting you do just to collect information or detail. It is used later at home or in the studio for a finished rendering.
Atmosphere Sketch—A drawing or painting you make to capture the atmosphere and mood for the finished work. You use it later for atmosphere and mood information, or as inspiration for an indoor painting.
Specific Sketch—A drawing or painting of a specific subject that has as much information, detail and atmosphere as possible. The sketch becomes the basis

S = SUN   B = BLUE
R = RED   Y = YELLOW
P.F. = PLOUGHED FIELD
GR = GREEN   W = WARM
P = PALE   GREY.
D = DARK   C = COLD

New Forest Ponies
14 MAY 77

COWS OVER GARDEN FENCE, MOTCOMBE
29 MAY 81

BEER FISHING BEACH
11 OCT

for a finished studio painting. The specific sketch is really a combination of information and atmosphere sketches. The only difference is that you go to a *specific place* to record what you see and feel. You then use all the information for a larger studio painting.

Notice that I've defined these types of sketches as the beginning or intermediate phases of a finished work. But it doesn't have to be that way. All sketches, whether they are drawings or paintings, can be considered "finished" works. Remember, that is in the eye of the beholder. In fact, some artists' sketches are preferred to their finished paintings.

Let us now look in more detail at the different types of sketches. Because each has its own purpose, you may have a preconceived idea of what type of sketch you are going to do before you go out. If you haven't, then go out and do an enjoyment sketch. Get your sketching equipment and go, looking at your surroundings with your sketchbook in hand. You have the perfect excuse to wander around and enjoy the atmosphere or beauty of your surroundings, no matter where you are.

As you observe before and during the sketching, everything will be stored in your visual memory. The resultant sketch becomes a trigger that brings a picture flooding back in seconds.

The sketch is also an everlasting visible reference to keep as you would a diary, or to use for information at a later date. An enjoyment sketch contains information even if it only shows how good—or bad—your technique was. In such cases you may want to use it to improve your next sketch. At other times, it might only remind you of that day's experiences. Therefore it doesn't matter how poor your technique was. If sketching gives you enjoyment, it's worthwhile.

ENJOYMENT SKETCH

The illustration on page 8 is a typical enjoyment sketch of mine. A few years ago I was in bed suffering from a slipped disc. It had never happened to me before, and I was furious. On the second day of being in bed, I couldn't do any serious work due to the pain, but I wanted to draw for the sheer delight of it. With the aid of a mirror my wife had propped up on the bed for me, I sketched myself. I was not aware of the scowl on my face as I drew it, but when I look at the sketch now, it makes me realize what my family had to put up with for nearly two weeks!

Just by having a pencil and sketchbook with you all the time, you can enjoy yourself anywhere. For example, I sometimes sketch while waiting in my car in a parking lot, page 11. Just 10 productive minutes can yield an enjoyment sketch.

INFORMATION SKETCH

The information sketch is self-explanatory. You make it to collect visual information to be used later in the studio, usually for a larger picture. Naturally you will have your own ideas on what information you need from such a sketch. However, it is no good going home and leaving your subject without

Chichester Cathedral, Sussex, 16-1/2x11-1/2 inches.

enough information, because you may never see it again. When in doubt record as much as practical.

Here are some of the things to remember to put in your sketch: the positions of the sun and shadows; the sizes and positions of important areas, such as a boats, buildings, trees, people and their positions relative to each other. All are so important that I have written a section on how to *measure from life* and transfer it to paper. It starts on page 38.

Also make sure you put something in your sketch to give an idea of scale. On page 8, in the drawing of two elm trees, scale is shown by the sheep and figure. The specific information represented here is of the trees, not the sheep or figure. Otherwise, I would have drawn them larger and, of course, in greater detail. Incidentally, on the facing page of my sketchbook I had made a note that the first area of foliage from the bottom of the trunk was half as tall as the tree. It was an important observation, but I didn't notice it before I completed the drawing!

If you are working in black and white prior to working in color, then you will need to make color notes. You can make yourself a code. For example, I use *DG* for dark green, *LR* for light red, and so on. Coding is very important. A week later when you look at your sketch, it is easy to forget whether a roof was red or blue.

I have worked from a sketch 10 years old to help me recall the scene. My visual memory told me the type of sky and atmosphere of that day, but color details are forgotten completely. I use the color code to tell me that.

Of course, when you do a watercolor sketch, don't put any comments or coding on it. Because you make a watercolor sketch in a relaxed manner, some can turn out to be beautiful on their own. You don't want to ruin your efforts with color codes. If you need color codes or notes to yourself, put them lightly on the back in pencil.

On page 9 I have put together sketches from some of my sketchbooks, but I have also added a code of important items for those of you who have not used one before. If you use this code, it will soon become second nature. Add your own, but keep the list short. Otherwise, your sketch will be hidden in letters.

ATMOSPHERE SKETCH

In an atmosphere sketch your most important goal is the feel of the subject in its environment. If you were sketching a city scene, the type of day—warm, windy, rainy, cold and so on—is not the only important atmospheric component. You must also capture such things as the mood of the streets, whether busy or quiet, wind-blown leaves, tree-lined pavements, and so on.

The only way to learn to sketch is to do it! If you sketch at every opportunity, you'll soon improve.

I suppose you could say that it is an information sketch gathering information about the atmosphere. But, in general, the detail is not there. You leave that to your imagination or to another sketch.

A BRIEF DIGRESSION

Before I discuss the specific sketch, I want to discuss actually leaving home and going out sketching. The most important item is *you*. You must have enough clothing to be warm. You can't relax and work outside if you are cold. For best results you must be comfortable and warm. You can always take clothing off to cool off, but you can't put more on if you don't have it with you.

Starting on page 18, I cover necessary equipment. Basically, you should take what you need, but try to take as little as possible. So for now let's consider what to draw when you get outside. If you are like me, you know that you are going out to sketch and therefore have a preconceived idea of what you want to draw. When you get to your starting point and you can't find what you had in mind, you get frustrated.

The only answer is to empty your mind completely of preconceived notions and look around at what's there. Usually, within minutes, you will discover an interesting subject in your surroundings.

But then comes the next obstacle—one I still have a problem with. You see a spot and think, "That's it!" But then you think it may be better around the corner, so you go to the next spot and think the same thing. And so it goes until you run out of corners and views, and an hour later you find your way back to the point you first started from.

I'm not exaggerating because I have done it. Self-discipline is essential if you are to stay at your first spot. The best solution to this dilemma is to stop when you see something interesting. If you say to yourself, "I like that," sketch it!

SPECIFIC SKETCH

I have left the specific sketch until last because in a way it embodies the other three—you should enjoy it and record information and atmosphere. The main difference is that the place and time are usually dictated to you. This means planning.

In painting the French beach below, my most important consideration was the planning. Although I was on vacation with my family, I knew that I would be doing a specific sketch for the book. We had a cottage only 200 yards from the beach, and after looking at the beach, I decided that it was a fine scene for my sketch.

I didn't do anything the first day because I wanted to get the feel of the place and try to decide on the most inspiring view. I wasn't surprised that the first view that inspired me was the one I decided to paint. The only problem I had was with the tide. Should it be in or out? I decided that it would be much more interesting to sketch when it was out. This would add more interest from people and the exposed rocks.

For the first sketch at the top of page 13, I used a 2B pencil and a large sketchbook of smooth, heavy paper. I started on the right side with the cliffs and rocks and progressed over to the left side.

I made this photograph of the beach from my sketching position. Compare it to the other illustrations to see how I changed the scene on paper.

It was very hot, but I wore a hat. Somewhere among the pencil dots in the water my son and my wife are swimming. I had no problems with this sketch. Everything went as planned, including the group of people to the right.

The next day I planned to sketch the same scene in watercolor to record the color. I also wanted to paint the scene with the tide up in case I changed my mind when I got back home. It was another hot day, but a cool breeze was blowing off the land, so I settled down at the back of the beach out of the cool breeze.

I had just set up and organized everything with a

Brittany Beach, 20x15 inches, watercolor. This was done at the beach.

This is how the original pencil sketch (23x9 inches) turned out.

board on my knees holding the 15x20-inch paper. But within minutes I was surrounded by people settling in for a day on the beach. Soon, there were umbrellas, folding chairs, bags, children, dogs and more distractions. If I had done a bit more planning, I would have expected it. I must have found the spot everyone wanted because within minutes I couldn't see the water and low rocks—just suntanned bodies only feet away from my sketchbook!

There was only one thing to do. Naturally I didn't want to pack up again and walk in the heat to the middle of the beach. But I did it anyway and once I was settled in, everything was perfect. I used a sheet of 140-pound, cold-pressed watercolor paper and drew in the picture with an HB pencil.

The tide was coming in, and I left the water line until I was ready to paint in the sea. I started with the sky, then worked down the rocks, leaving the paper white where people were to go in. Then I painted in the sea, which had come up further since I started to draw it. After that I put in the people, the boat and the beach.

Poor planning led to another problem—running children and dogs kicking up sand as they ran past. I had to keep covering and uncovering my paints with a plastic bag, so the painting took longer than expected. I also took a photograph of the beach to help you see what changes were made to the sketches.

Back in England I used the painted sketch to make a finished painting. I used acrylic paints on a 16x24-inch canvas. It's shown below. Because of my sketching experiences, I felt as if I had known that beach all my life.

Brittany Beach, 24x16 inches, acrylic. This is the final painting done in my studio. The pencil and watercolor sketches were invaluable.

Basic Perspective

You don't need to know all about perspective to be able to paint or sketch a picture. However, it's my opinion that knowing a few basics will make your sketching easier and the results more convincing. I think most people are somewhat familiar with the terms *horizon, eye level* and *vanishing point,* so I'll start there.

When you look out to sea, the horizon will always be at eye level, whether you are on a cliff top or lying flat on the sand.

If you are in a room, there won't be a horizon, but you still have an eye-level view. To find it, hold a pencil horizontally in front of your eyes at arm's length. Eye level is where the pencil seems to hit the opposite wall.

If two parallel lines were marked out on the ground and extended to the horizon, they would visually converge at the vanishing point. This is why railroad tracks seem to get closer together the farther away they are. They "meet" at the vanishing point.

To some people, these basic principles of perspective come naturally. For others it is hard work. But unless you are going to draw complicated buildings or other large, intricate things, don't let perspective rules worry you when you sketch. You will actually "use" perspective in the same way you do for the examples on the opposite page.

The examples on the opposite page will make basic principles clear and eventually effortless. Don't let the technical appearance of the examples intimidate you. Just draw them yourself step-by-step in the order discussed here. It's much easier than it looks. I drew these freehand on tracing paper with a technical drawing pen. I used a felt-tip pen for the thick lines.

At the top of the page I drew the eye level. Then I drew a square (A) and put a mark to the left at eye level. The mark became the vanishing point. The object is to make the square (A) into a box. Draw a line from the vanishing point to both left corners of the square (B) and then do the same to the right corners (C). This determines two sides of the box.

Next draw a line between the top and bottom guidelines parallel to the left side of the square. See points a and b. This gives one side of the box (D). Then draw a horizontal line from point a to touch the guideline on the other side of the box. Do the same again starting at b and draw a horizontal line to the lower guideline. Finally, join the points oppo-

site a and b with a perpendicular line (D).

This yields the box, drawn in perspective. Essentially you've made a two-dimensional drawing appear three dimensional. Using basic principles of perspective, such as eye level and vanishing points, gives the box the appearance of depth.

By adding a roof to the box, I turned the box into a house (E). I added the roof by first finding the center of the initial square. The center is where the diagonals of the square intersect. This principle works for rectangles too. From the center I drew a vertical guideline up to meet another line drawn from the vanishing point to the point of the roof. Where these two lines cross determines the peak of the roof. Finish the roof by drawing parallel lines from the upper-left corner of the square and point a to the guideline representing the roof peak.

I did drawings A through E with a square seen straight on. But there are other ways to do it too. For example, in F the house on the corner has two vanishing points. One is at the left and the other at the right. The principle is the same as for the first house you drew, except the lines on *both sides* of the house meet at a vanishing point.

I have put more buildings into this drawing to show you how a street is built up—two streets in fact. One goes to the left and the other to the right. Because the house on the right with the chimney is seen straight on, its other sides aren't shown.

In drawing G I have drawn a "bird's eye view" of the same scene. All I did was change eye level by putting it higher than the initial houses.

Drawing H is just the opposite—a "worm's eye view." Eye level and vanishing point are very low—at the bottom edge of the drawing. In fact, they are at ground level.

In all of these drawings, notice how *all* lines that are parallel in real life meet at the vanishing point. This includes windows, window sills, doors, gutters, street lights and pavement. In drawing F there is even a guideline for the top of the chimney.

When I sketch, especially if I am doing buildings and man-made objects, I start adding the elements of perspective by first finding eye level. I do it by holding my pencil horizontally at arm's length in front of my eyes. Where it "touches" the objects in the scene becomes eye level. I then draw it in on my sketch pad, position the center of interest, and work from there.

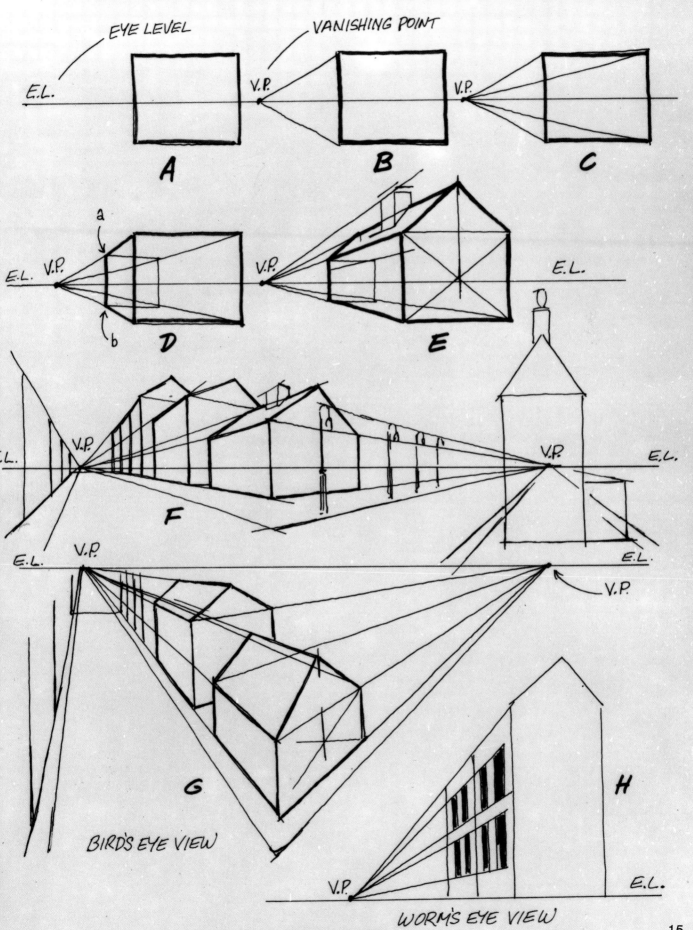

EYE LEVEL

VANISHING POINT

E.L.

V.P.

V.P.

A

B

C

a

E.L.

V.P.

V.P.

E.L.

b

D

E

E.L.

V.P.

V.P.

E.L.

F

E.L.

E.L.

V.P.

V.P.

BIRD'S EYE VIEW

G

H

V.P.

E.L.

WORM'S EYE VIEW

Elementary Composition

11-1/2x9-inch information sketch.

11-1/2x8-1/2-inch information sketch.

Composition is mostly a matter of personal observation and taste, so it is difficult to say exactly what is good composition or bad. If we like a picture, it is tough to know how much the composition influences us. Perhaps the subject or colors are most appealing.

My definition of *composition* is the way you position elements of the scene on paper to convey a visual message to the viewer. It's a special subject requiring a lot of study. For sketching purposes, we'll keep it simple with some basic rules. From there, you should let your instincts guide you.

I'll start with a very old rule I was taught in art school. Although it is a good rule of thumb to use, don't stick with it too rigidly. Be willing to deviate from it to create a more personal style. Sometimes, this will yield a more unusual and better picture.

In the drawing at the top of page 17, I divided a rectangle into thirds, vertically and horizontally. The lines cross at points A, B, C and D, creating *focal points*. If your center of interest is positioned on or near a focal point, then you should have a good composition.

For example, look at the people standing on the cliff at focal point A on the opposite page. The composition "works"—at least it does according to the rule. Now look at the sketch below it, in which the two figures on the cliff are in the center of the picture. Compared to the sketch above, it looks less interesting and lively.

The other sketches at the bottom of page 17 show simple compositions using different focal points. This is one way to change composition by using the center of interest. You can also do it by making the center of interest different from its immediate surroundings—for example, with tonal contrasts in black and white or color contrasts in color.

When sketching a landscape or seascape, always place the horizon above or below the center of the paper, never in the middle. Then place the center of interest at your chosen focal point. Start working away from it.

If you observe nature carefully, you will find that its lines—hedges, rivers, roads and so on—will help to bring the picture together and form a natural composition. For now, put in everything you see. Later experience will tell you what, if anything, to

As described in the text, a detailed information sketch usually offers more than one composition for a finished work. This is why it's important to include as much information as practical in the sketch.

leave out. Don't be tempted to distort a view to get more on your sketchbook. If you do, the composition of elements will look wrong.

Look at the drawing at the top of this page. When I sketched it, I did not intend to make a picture. The

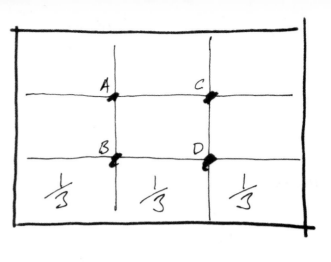

elements were just information sketches put together on a page of my pad. The same is true of the chicken sketches. This is not composed in any way.

The object right now is to get as much information as possible. This is what I have done in the sketch at the bottom of page 16. I started the island in the middle of my sketchbook and worked on both sides of it. This gave me enough room to put on the information I needed to be able to work from it at home.

At home I can recompose to my heart's content. In fact, the sketch yields two different compositions for a painting. The blue outline shows a picture with the island as the center of interest. The red outline gives a different view. The foreground figures become the center of interest and are at a different focal point. If the information you want when you go out relates to composition, then naturally your information sketch should be drawn with composition in mind.

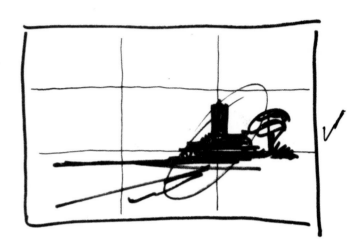

Suppose your subject is large, such as a landscape or a village square, and you can't decide which part to sketch. In this case, cut a 4x6-inch rectangle out of a thin piece of cardboard. This is called a *mask*. You can make a proportional mask the same size as a page in your sketchbook. Then the view you see through it will fit your sketchbook exactly. There's more information on proportions on page 44.

Hold up your mask at arm's length and look, with one eye closed, through the "window." Move it around slowly up and down, and backward and forward until you see a good "picture" in view, as in the illustration above. Make mental notes of where your arm is and where the key points of the scene hit the inside edge of the mask. Mark these on your sketch pad and away you go.

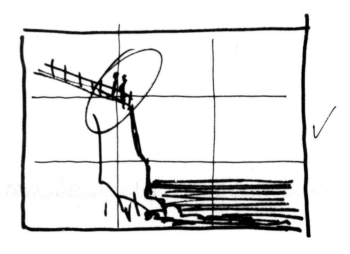

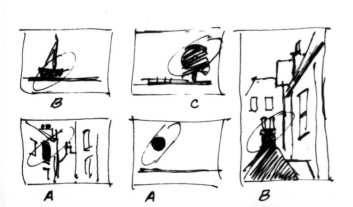

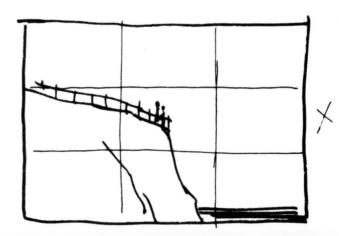

Equipment

The equipment you need for sketching can be much simpler than what you may need for painting. Even so, some people—including me—like to collect a wide variety of different materials. Perhaps that's part of being an artist. For example, I have an oil painting palette that I have had since art school and enough brushes to paint the hull of an ocean liner. I never seem able to throw away my old equipment because I'm sure that I'll eventually find a use for it later.

One way to justify such actions is to buy good equipment. In fact, I recommend that you buy the best you can afford. The equipment will last longer, make sketching easier, and no doubt help you produce better results.

BLACK-AND-WHITE SKETCHING MATERIALS

In so-called black-and-white sketching, black is typically the drawing or painting medium; white is the paper it is worked on. Photos on page 19 show different materials you can use for black-and-white sketching. On the following pages, I discuss using them specifically.

Pencils—In my opinion, the most important piece of equipment is the lowly pencil. Not surprisingly, we tend to take the pencil for granted. Everybody has pencils, and we've all used them since childhood. But let's take a closer look at the pencil. There's a lot more to it than you might think.

A good brand of drawing pencil uses about 13 different types of lead. The middle one is the most common for everyday use. Typically, it's labeled *HB* on the side of the pencil. The *B* represents the degree of lead softness and darkness. The higher the number rating in front of the B, the softer and darker the lead. Ratings are B, 2B, 3B, 4B, 5B and 6B, the softest.

The *H* stands for the hardness of the lead. The higher the H rating, the harder and lighter the pencil lead. H ratings include H, 2H, 3H, 4H, 5H and 6H, the hardest. For general-purpose sketching, all you need are HB and 2B pencils. After using these for a while, try some others to see which pencils feel best. The photo at right shows different tones that you can produce using HB, 2B and 6B pencils.

When you sharpen the pencil as shown above, use a sharp knife and cut off controlled, positive "slices" to make a long, gradual taper to the lead. This way, you can see the point easily when you are sketching. The second photo above shows two

A razor knife is a good pencil sharpener. You could also use a sharp pocket knife.

The left and middle points are best for sketching.

Protect your sharpened pencils when you put together a sketching set.

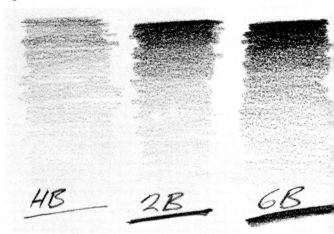

Different leads yield different tonal effects.

kinds of sharpenings—a sharp point and a flat chisel. The latter is good for shading and making broad strokes. The third pencil is sharpened incorrectly.

There are two ways to protect sharpened pencil points when you take them out sketching. As shown, you can band them to a piece of thick cardboard or plastic. The other way is to make a cover for the lead out of heavy paper and masking tape.

Pencils offer a variety of other helpful features. For example, some pencils are round and smooth. Some are hexagonal for a different "feel" when held. Some pencils come with thick leads; some have thin leads. Generally, the thinner the lead the harder the pencil, and vice-versa. Pencil manufacturers may also color code their pencils so you can easily choose the pencil you need without having to look for the lead rating on the side.

As shown below, there are many materials you can use for black-and-white sketching. But if you are just starting, don't think that you need all of them. Rather, start with only one pencil or pen. Stay with it until your sketching is good. Then you'll be able to use some of the other materials described here.

Pencil-like Materials—The photo at left shows pencil-like materials. Technically not all are pencils. In addition to standard pencils, you see charcoal sticks, charcoal pencils, conté pencils, conté crayons, and a box of pastels. You also see essential materials, such as a sketchbook, drawing papers, kneadable eraser and spray fixative.

Ink Materials—The photo at right shows ink materials for sketching—a bottle of black India ink, fountain-pen ink, pen holder and nibs, palette for diluting ink with water, sable brush, fountain pen, ballpoint pen, technical drawing pen, felt-tip pens, sketchbooks and blotting paper.

Sketchbook—The size of the sketchbook you choose is up to you. I have different sizes for different purposes. If I am going out on a sketching trip or to do a complicated information sketch, I take the largest sketchbook I work with. It's about 12x16 inches. I use a smaller one for general use because it's easier to carry. My smallest is about 6x9 inches. I keep it in my car. If the situation is right and something is in view to sketch, the pad is always there. If you do the same, don't forget to always stash a couple pencils in the car too.

If your pad is too small to rest your drawing hand, you need a support for the pad. I have seen students standing up holding a *small* pad in one hand and drawing with the other. Their drawing hand can never rest. It is tough enough to draw standing up, but even worse if you can't rest your hand on the drawing surface from time to time.

COLOR SKETCHING MATERIALS

The same principles apply to working in color as in black and white—you can have as many or as few materials as you want.

Pastels—These are soft, chalky pigments in the form of a stubby cylinder. They yield soft, smooth colors. Pastels are available in more than 50 different colors. Each is available in a few tints, making nearly 200 pastels available.

The best way to start a collection of colors is to

Pencil sketching set.

Ink sketching set.

buy a box of 12 or 36 soft pastels that are chosen for landscapes. One is shown on the bottom of the page. I have used such pastels for all the exercises in this book. When you get used to the medium, you can then buy different tints, colors or refill pastels individually.

When using pastels, you will need some paper or a pastel sketchpad with a selection of colored sheets. Also use some fixative, a bristle brush for rubbing out areas of pastel, a kneadable eraser, an HB or 2B pencil, and a rag for cleaning your hands.

Watercolors—You can buy watercolors in tubes, or in kits of various sizes. I do not recommend tubes for beginners because they are difficult to control. Kits are easier to control and come in different sizes. Colors in my kits are Payne's gray, burnt umber, Hooker's green No. 1, ultramarine blue, alizarin crimson, yellow ochre, cerulean blue, burnt sienna, cadmium red, raw umber, raw sienna, and cadmium yellow pale.

The photo below shows the basic sketching set for watercolor work. Start with two round sable brushes—a No. 10 and a No. 6. The quality you get will depend on the price you pay. You also need a paintbox to hold 12 pans of color or 12 half pans. The one in front holds whole pans. The one in back is smaller, but holds more colors and also carries a water supply. It's ideal for putting in your pocket or handbag.

Also bring along HB and 2B pencils, a kneadable eraser that will not smudge, a drawing board with watercolor paper or a watercolor sketch pad, blotting

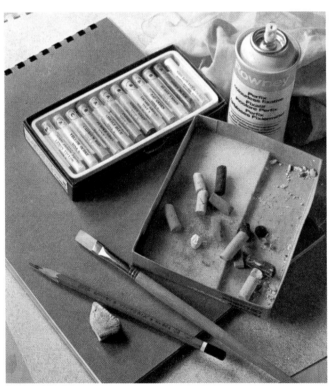

Pastel sketching set.

Watercolor sketching set.

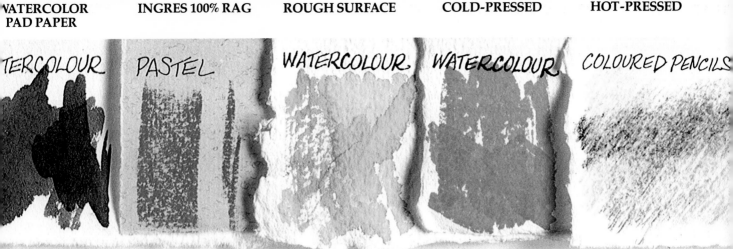

paper, a sponge and a water jar. I also suggest that you carry a tube of white paint with your equipment. I use designers' gouache.

Brushes—In painting, the brush is the most important tool. Like the pencil in a pencil sketch, a brush is the link between what you see and what goes on the paper. Therefore, be happy with those you choose. In addition to the No. 6 and No. 10 I've recommended, consider using a No. 1 or No. 2 for making thin lines.

The photo below shows how these three brushes and others compare in terms of size. Nylon brushes are less expensive. To make large, watercolor washes, use a large flat brush such as the large, fat squirrel-hair wash brush.

Paper—This subject is so broad that I cannot give a complete explanation in the limited space available here. Instead, I've shown a selection above to give you an idea of some basic differences. These specific papers are suitable for black-and-white and color work. They are reproduced actual size and indicate the paper and medium used.

For pencil work, a smooth paper is normally used. Heavy, smooth drawing or writing paper has a slight tooth, making it an all-purpose sketching surface. You can buy sketchpads of all sizes composed of these papers. Heavy tracing paper is ideal for pencil work or felt-tip pens because it won't let ink spread. Another paper good with ink is bristol board. It's smooth and coated on both sides. You may also want to use it for Rotring, pencil, conté and watercolor washes.

You can use just about any paper for color sketching, but the best for watercolors is handmade and comes in three distinct surfaces—rough, cold-pressed and hot-pressed. Rough-surface paper is self-explanatory. Cold-pressed paper—my main choice—has less grain, or texture, than rough surface. Hot-pressed paper has the smoothest surface of the three.

Ingres is a brand of 100% rag paper. Other brands of 100% rag are available too, so check with your local art-supply store. This type of paper is ideal for pastel work. Typically, it's made in various tints. It too can be found in sketchbook form.

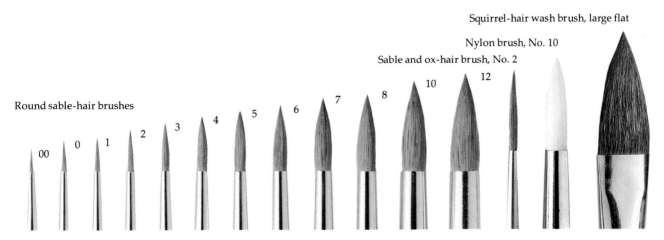

These brushes are shown actual size. Some brush series have additional sizes to those shown.

Sketching In Black And White

Now I can start showing you how to use various black-and-white materials. You'll see that they can be inexpensive, handy and a lot of fun.

In the how-to photos showing my sketching hand you'll see two different kinds of arrows. The solid arrow shows the direction of the strokes. The outlined arrow shows the direction in which the pencil travels over the paper. I use this method throughout the book.

Simple pencil sketching set.

Pencil

With pencil sketching, all you really need are one pencil, an eraser and a sketchpad, as shown at top. For me, this is the most versatile and pleasing way to sketch. It is also one of the least expensive. More than half of my outdoor sketching is done with this equipment.

When we pick up a pencil, it's usually for writing. Holding a pencil this way, however, is not ideal for sketching. It limits you to careful line work and is called the *short drawing position*. For a freer and more fluid motion, necessary when you are making a large sketch, hold the pencil at least three inches from the point. Use the pencil at a flatter angle to the paper than when you write. This *long drawing position* gives your strokes more versatility.

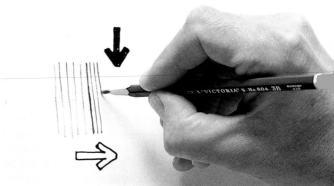

Short drawing position.

The bottom photo shows the *flat drawing position*—a totally different way to hold your pencil. It is almost flat on the paper, held off by your thumb and index finger. This allows you to lightly touch and skim the surface. The results are fast, broad strokes because the long edge of the lead yields large, shaded areas.

These are just three main ways to hold a pencil. There are many other variations. Start with these three and you'll eventually discover variations. Practice whenever you can, even if you are just doodling. Don't worry about drawing. Get used to using a pencil to create on paper.

Long drawing position.
Flat drawing position.

On the opposite page are some pencil sketches from my sketchbooks. They are reproduced smaller than actual size. The only one not made especially for this book is in the lower-right corner. It shows doodles, indicating what a single pencil can do. When you practice, try using at least three tones with white paper.

DARK
2B pencil

MEDIUM

LIGHT

PRACTICE

MIKE

Ink and Wash

Using a single ink pen and an ink pen with wash are two old and traditional ways of drawing and sketching. In the former, just the ink pen is the drawing instrument. In the latter, you use a brush along with an ink pen. The brush adds ink, either undiluted or diluted with water, to achieve different tonal values in wash form over the lines. This results in quick tonal variations.

If you use black India drawing ink, never put a brush with water into the ink. Always use a separate *palette,* the small round plastic dish shown in the photo. Put a brush full of ink into the palette. Then use water to thin ink on the palette. Think of it as watercolor painting with just one color.

At right in the top photo is a *pen holder.* It holds a *nib,* also called a *pen point.* Typically you use a pen holder and nib to draw fine lines. Nibs are available in a large variety of shapes and sizes. You use this type of pen in a dip-and-draw fashion. For sketching, this means that you must take a bottle of ink, water, and a palette and brush if you intend to work with wash. With washes, you must use water-proof drawing ink with the pen. Otherwise, the fine lines will smear and run during the wash. You need a hard paper or board for fine nib work, such as bristol board.

Nibs are not expensive, so try different ones to get the feel of working with them. Don't be afraid of them—they are more flexible and stronger than you might think. Even so, you can damage a nib if you press hard on an upstroke.

A *fountain pen* is at left in the top photo. Such a pen has a less ''scratchy'' feel. It flows over the board or paper more readily than ''dip-in'' pens. It also has the advantage of not having to be dipped in ink every few minutes, therefore you don't have to carry a bottle of ink and risk spilling it. A fountain pen works well on a greater variety of papers too. For example, smooth heavy drawing paper is great with a fountain pen.

The bottom two photos show how you can vary line thickness by just altering the direction of stroke.

A specialized type of fountain pen is the *technical drawing pen*—the red pen in the above photo. Two brands are Rapidograph and Kohinoor. Special ink is necessary because the pen uses a very fine tube to deliver ink to the tiny point. Different sizes of points are available. The main disadvantage with this type of pen is that you have to hold it upright for it to work properly. Even so, it's worth trying one to see if you like it for freehand sketching.

On the opposite page are a variety of sketches done with ink. Large solid areas were done with brush washes. At lower right are some examples of lines and tones you can achieve with either a pen or brush.

Simple ink sketching set.

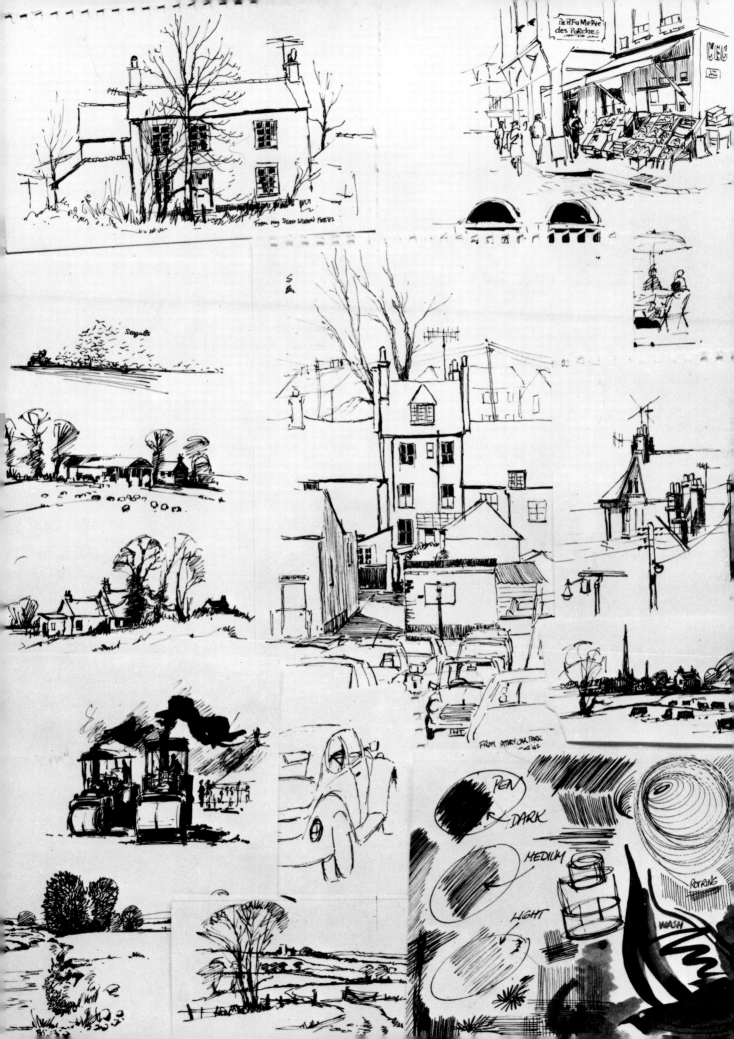

PaRFuMeRie
des PoRChes

CEG

From my Studio Window FEB 82

S
Bu

Seagulls

FROM OTTERY OAK PARK
-82 '42

PEN
DARK
MEDIUM
LIGHT
ROTRING
WASH

Charcoal, Conté and Pastel

Charcoal is not a medium for the neat and fussy sketcher. It is for broad, adventurous sketching, in which one stroke of the charcoal can cover inches of paper for a certain effect. It is most exciting to use for atmosphere sketches of landscapes. Skies and large masses of landscape go on the paper quickly.

Charcoal comes in different grades in either pencil form or as individual sticks. You have more freedom using a stick because you can use the long edge for broad shading, but a pencil is cleaner and easier to use. It is not the simplest medium to work with and doesn't suit everybody.

Because it can smudge, you will have to practice working with your hand *not* resting on the paper. This is very difficult to get used to, but like most things it is worth trying to get results you like. You will find that by sketching without resting your hand, you may become freer and more spontaneous. Also, detail is minimized. For some of us this can be one way of getting out of the habit of being too concerned about details.

Charcoal can be worked on almost any paper, but I suggest you start on smooth drawing paper. Naturally, work on other surfaces too until you find one that suits you. After sketching, "fix" your work with a spray fixative. This will stop it from smudging and preserve it for years.

The above photo also shows conté pencils. They are similar to charcoal pencils but are harder. Though harder, they too will smudge, so the same warnings apply. Conté pencils are also available in white and red. Experiment using white and black conté on a gray paper.

Finally, there is a tonal set of artists' soft pastels. Tones range from black to white. Essentially, a sketching set with these is similar to what you need for colored pastels, except that you don't need colored paper.

With these materials an eraser isn't used much. This is because it is difficult to erase smudgy lines. Be sure to bring the spray fixative with you. It will be the only bulky part of your charcoal sketch kit.

You can have lots of fun with these smudgy materials. Use them the next time you want to try very quick sketching.

Charcoal, conté pencil and pastel sketching set.

CHARCOAL

DARK

MEDIUM

LIGHT

CONTÉ

DARK

MEDIUM

LIGHT

Felt-tip and Ballpoint Pens

One thing is certain, the old masters didn't use these materials. I sometimes wonder what they would have to say about them? Would they have used them? I think so because felt-tip and ballpoint pens are excellent for sketching.

The one disadvantage of the ballpoint pen is that a sketch made with one looks a bit too "mechanical." This is because there is not much line variation possible, especially if you compare it with a pencil line.

But, consider its advantages: It is inexpensive. You don't have to dip it in ink or fill it. You can get black and many colors. You can get different grades of line with different brands of pen. If you are miles from anywhere, the chances of it not working are remote. You can work with it on almost any surface. And you probably have one nearby, no matter where you are.

The basic disadvantages are that its performance is limited, and the ink is not easily erased. But if you can accept these, a ballpoint pen is a fine sketching tool. Personally, I consider them as good emergency tools, but not my preferred choice.

Felt-tip pens have more "character" in their lines because you can vary stroke width. In addition, points come in a wider range of sizes, from very fine to very broad. Points can be fine and sharp, blunt or chisel-shaped. Lines possible from the latter two are illustrated at right. Any good art-supply store will surprise you with the number of colors and sizes of felt-tip pens available.

Hold and use a felt-tip pen designed for writing as you would a pencil. It can give results just as good. Generally, you can work with it on any paper that you would with pencil. Remember, there is no rubbing out with a ballpoint or felt-tip pen. This means that you are forced to carefully observe the subject before drawing any lines on paper. If you draw some lines that are wrong, don't start again. Work over them unless most of the lines are really wrong!

My examples are on the opposite page. Doodles are at bottom right. Now I have described many different tools for drawing in black and white. Among them is bound to be a couple that suits you. Try them until you find your favorite. Scribble, scratch and scrawl on paper after paper until you know what you can get from your chosen drawing instrument.

Felt-tip and ballpoint pens sketching set.

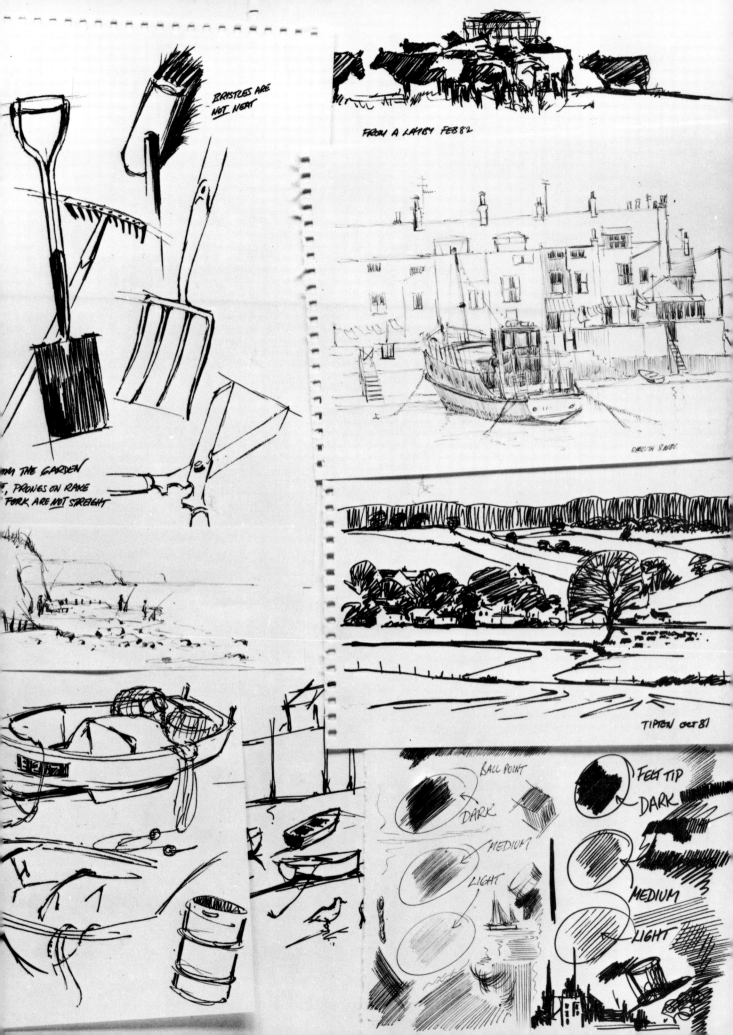

BRISTLES ARE
NOT NEAT

FROM A LATBY FEB 82

ROM THE GARDEN
, PRONGS ON RAKE
FORK ARE NOT STREIGHT

EXMOUTH 8 NOV.

TIPTON OCT 81

BALL POINT

DARK

MEDIUM

LIGHT

FELT TIP
DARK

MEDIUM

LIGHT

Exercises In Black And White

Before starting these simple exercises, you should have practiced and experimented with black-and-white sketching materials. By now you should understand the main characteristics of the tools.

All the sketches on these two pages are reproduced half actual size. They were done in stages to show you how I work. The stages are simulated—I have simply drawn each a few times with more elements in each successive stage. But in the six exercises starting on page 48, each stage is of the *same* sketch, which was photographed as I drew it. This shows what was put into the sketch and how it progressed from start to finish.

The two exercises below will help you in the use of broad pencil strokes. To duplicate the exercises, use a 3B pencil held in the flat drawing position. It will give broad shading for the tonal work, as shown on page 22.

Start the exercise at left by drawing in the line of the field. Then put in the buildings—the center of interest—and follow my stages. Proceed to the second exercise. Don't belabor your pencil work on these exercises. Develop free motions, trying for light against dark—strong contrast—with shading.

The sketch at the top of page 31 was done with a fountain pen. To duplicate it, let your pen be light and free. Don't be too technical, but follow the stages as I show them and you will get the "feel" of how a sketch builds.

If you like, you can try any of these sketches with other black-and-white materials. You may have more fun and better results than if you use the same materials as I did. Experimenting may also help you see which subjects suit which medium. For instance, it would be difficult to get the same atmosphere in the second exercise below if you used a fine-nibbed pen. The sky would be stratchy and difficult to make very black. But with charcoal pencils the atmosphere in the sketch would be effective.

The last exercise on the bottom of page 31 was done on heavy paper with a stick of charcoal. As I explained earlier, charcoal is for broad, adventurous treatment. Even so, this simple sketch shows how you can use it for fine work too. Work the trees from the bottom, upward and outward in the direction of their growth.

Consider these exercises as useful training, not joyless tasks. Copying these will help you to "copy" and observe nature when you are out sketching more personal subjects.

SKETCH THESE TWO IN BROAD TREATMENT WITH A 3B PENCIL

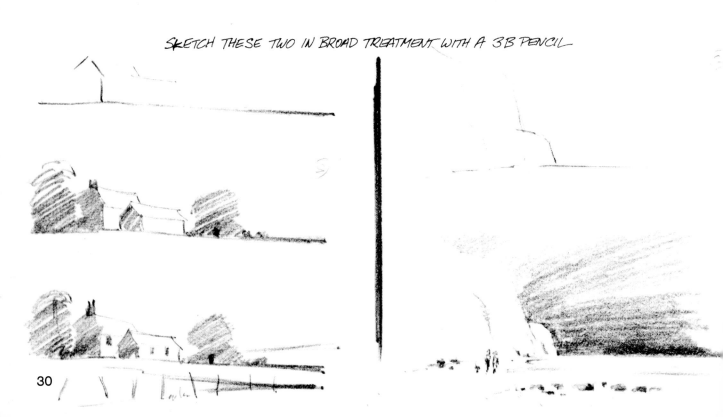

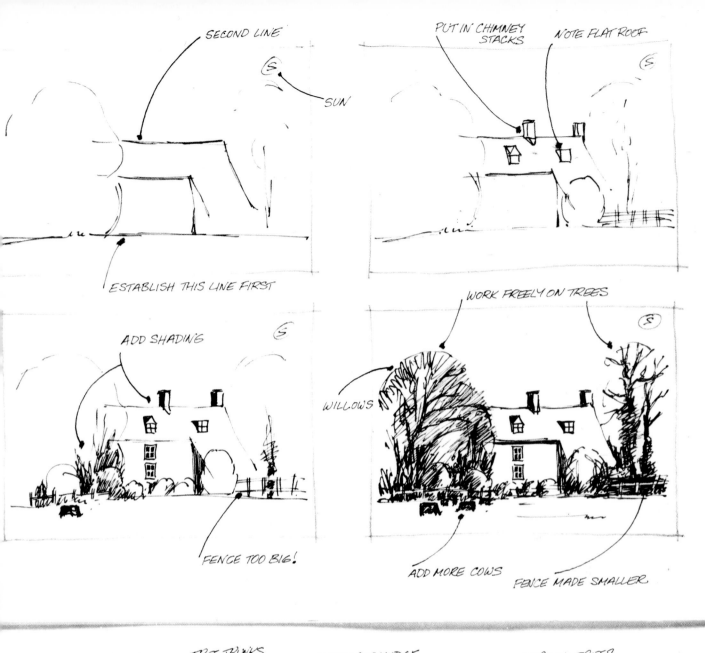

SECOND LINE

PUT IN CHIMNEY STACKS

NOTE FLAT ROOF

SUN

ESTABLISH THIS LINE FIRST

ADD SHADING

WORK FREELY ON TREES

WILLOWS

FENCE TOO BIG!

ADD MORE COWS

FENCE MADE SMALLER

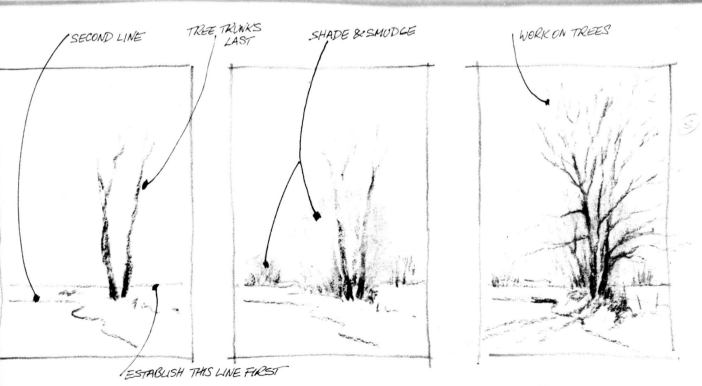

SECOND LINE

TREE TRUNKS LAST

SHADE & SMUDGE

WORK ON TREES

ESTABLISH THIS LINE FIRST

Sketching In Color

In this book I discuss sketching with watercolors and pastels. In the next few pages I give you good information and inspiration that will take some of the mystery out of using color sketching materials. If you want more information about these materials, I can cheerfully recommend two other books in this series: *How to Paint With Pastels* by John Blockley and *How to Paint With Watercolors* by Alwyn Crawshaw.

Watercolors

Color is all around us, all of the time. It can influence our emotions by being pleasing or depressing. Also, it can affect our senses by giving the effect of cold, warmth, dark or light. All of this is the result of just three *primary* colors—red, yellow and blue. In this book I use two sets of red, yellow and blue painter's primaries to give greater scope to color mixing, as shown on page 33.

Learning to mix colors to obtain a variety of different colors is an essential skill. The illustration on the opposite page shows just three examples. You can also control the tone of a color. In watercolor painting you use more water and less paint to lighten a color. To make it darker use more paint and less water.

The illustration shows how to mix a black. I like to do it this way because I think a mixed black looks "alive." However, many artists use a premixed black. You should too if you prefer it to a black you mix yourself.

Watercolor is a good medium to learn to paint with. Some people consider oil better because you can paint over or rub out your mistakes. This may be important for you, but I recommend that you start with watercolor rather than oils for two reasons:

1) Whether you are artistic or not, you probably first tried painting with watercolors or other water-based paint as a child. You probably used all types of paper too, from old typing paper to brown wrapping paper. For these reasons you won't be a complete novice if you start sketching with watercolors. This is probably not the case with oils.

2) Watercolor is a very convenient medium to use indoors to practice with. The equipment is easy to set up and use, and there is no disagreeable odor, as there can be with oils. I don't mind the smell of oils, but others in my house find it distasteful. Therefore I most often work with oils in my separate studio.

Once you have some experience painting with watercolors, color mixing and brush strokes, try oils if you like. Basically, you should stick with the medium that suits you best.

When you are out sketching with watercolor, try not to get too involved with mixing subtle colors. Deal with broad areas, using colors that are simple to mix. Time and experience will expand your color range.

When you are out in the country, look into the distance, covering up the foreground fields with your hands. Then look at the foreground fields. You'll notice that the color in the distance is bluer than the color in the foreground field. The foreground color will appear warmer and more realistic.

Look at a brick wall or a side of a red-brick house. The color is strong and bold. Now look at a brick wall or house in the same light but much farther away. The same red will appear paler and almost reddish-gray.

When you are out, look for these color changes. Paint them into your sketches and you will find that the background "stays" in the distance and the foreground in front. Your sketch will be subtle and

more realistic. When mixing colors to reproduce this phenomenon, add blue to make colors cooler; add red to make them warmer.

When you practice mixing colors indoors, look at the objects around you and try to match the colors. Remember that one color can look different against another. For example, if you are painting on white paper and the color is not quite right, paint the color next to the object in the sketch and you will probably see a difference. At this stage don't be overly concerned with shapes. Just paint splotches of color. Doodle as I have done at left.

Pastels

Try working with pastels in the same way. Mix the pastels into each other on paper to get the required colors. Because there are so many different shades of pastels available, mixing is not as important as it is with watercolors. Even so, you can mix pastels on paper to obtain different colors.

I suspect that you probably haven't used colored pencils since school, so why not try them for sketching? Some color mixing is possible, but is limited compared to watercolors and pastels. Look at my doodles.

To be able to finally paint your color sketches, you have to train yourself to observe color and put down your observations in the sketch. You can't do this overnight, but with practice you will probably do it sooner than you think.

PRIMARY COLORS

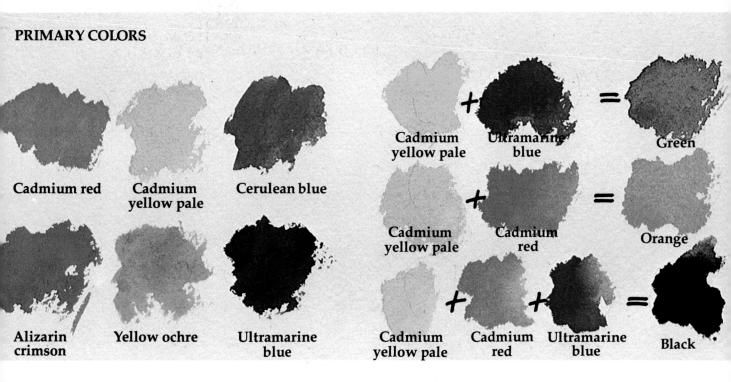

Cadmium red   Cadmium yellow pale   Cerulean blue

Alizarin crimson   Yellow ochre   Ultramarine blue

Cadmium yellow pale + Ultramarine blue = Green

Cadmium yellow pale + Cadmium red = Orange

Cadmium yellow pale + Cadmium red + Ultramarine blue = Black

Exercises In Color

Now that you have practiced color mixing and doodling, you will be ready to try some simple exercises. Don't let the exercises on these two pages worry you just because they have shape and form. In fact, they are composed of just a few simple colors. For instance, look at the small rowboat on the opposite page. The first stage gets its third dimension from the darker tone superimposed in the right places. Doing this requires careful *observation* of the subject, not necessarily great skill as a painter.

Take this concept a little further and look at the wheelbarrow. As you gain confidence, you will find that you can put the second tone in—the shadow side of the wheelbarrow—as you paint in the first stage. In other words, you could paint in the light area on two sides and then paint in the other two sides with a darker tone. In this way you skip a stage and superimpose less.

When you are painting complicated subjects, you will find that this happens throughout the picture. If you find similar shortcuts that enable you to work better, use them. Painting is very personal, so don't be afraid to develop your own special techniques.

Look at the illustrations on this page, starting at top. This is basically an atmosphere sketch in progress. Any detail needed could have been drawn on a separate piece of paper. I worked in flat, watercolor washes from the sky to the foreground.

I am not certain that the foreground shadows are absolutely correct, but they look good to me! I added them later at home to show how shadows create the illusion of flat ground. As you can see, I used only three main colors for this exercise. The fourth color, cadmium red, was used for the tiny buses in the distance. I worked on a sheet of cold-pressed watercolor paper.

The sketches on the opposite page were done on heavy drawing paper. All sketches in this section are reproduced half actual size.

Concentrate on working simply. This is especially important when you are out sketching. For example, the sketch of the church on page 36 was done with colored pencils on tracing paper. Only three colors and black were used. Black merely serves to tone down some of the colors and add some depth detail.

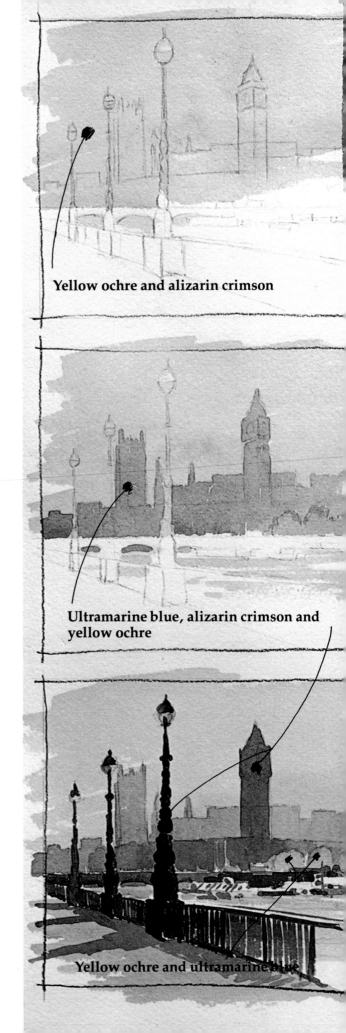

Yellow ochre and alizarin crimson

Ultramarine blue, alizarin crimson and yellow ochre

Yellow ochre and ultramarine blue

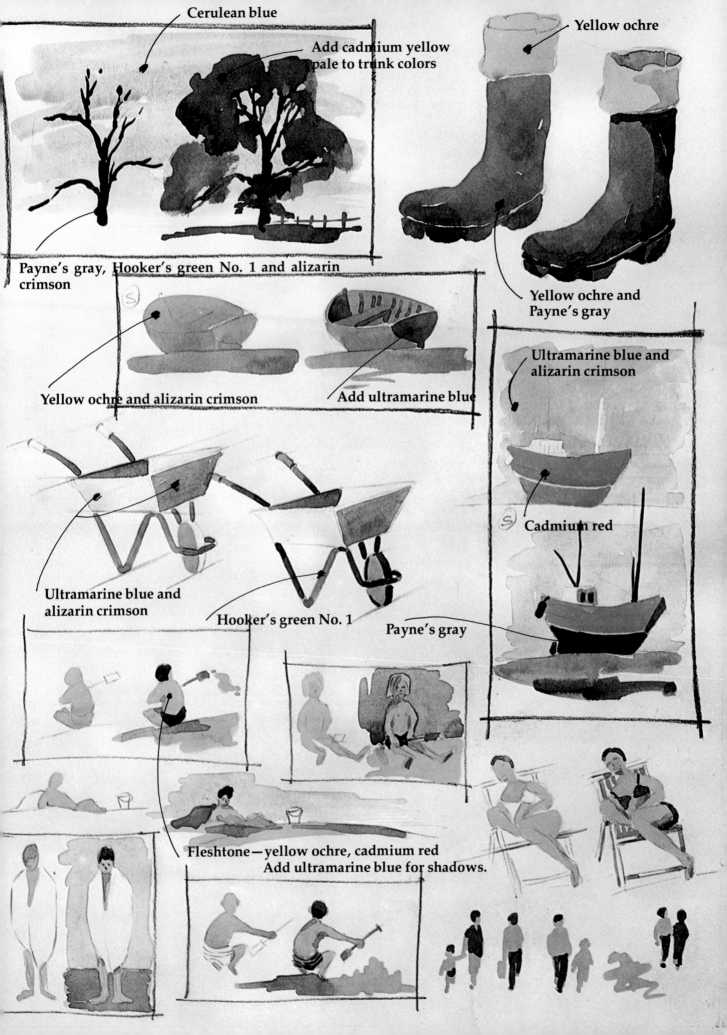

Cerulean blue

Add cadmium yellow pale to trunk colors

Yellow ochre

Payne's gray, Hooker's green No. 1 and alizarin crimson

Yellow ochre and Payne's gray

Yellow ochre and alizarin crimson

Add ultramarine blue

Ultramarine blue and alizarin crimson

Ultramarine blue and alizarin crimson

Cadmium red

Hooker's green No. 1

Payne's gray

Fleshtone—yellow ochre, cadmium red
Add ultramarine blue for shadows.

The sketch at the bottom of the page was made with pastels on layout paper. When I painted in the cows, I smudged them a bit with my finger and picked out more detail at the next stage. I added the sky and rubbed gently over the distant, snow-covered fields. This is an atmosphere sketch. If I had wanted details of cows, I would have drawn them in pencil first and made the sketch larger.

For the sketch at the top of page 37, I used a paper with a very rough surface and pale yellow color. I used only three watercolors and eventually finished off the sketch with a fountain pen.

In the sketch at the bottom of page 37 I used a smooth, heavy paper again. It is very important to get used to working watercolors on this type of paper because you may use the paper for a pencil or pen sketch and then want to add notes in watercolor.

I have worked very freely with this atmosphere sketch, but there would be enough information for me to work a larger picture from it in the studio. Never forget that you decide what your needs are for an information or atmosphere sketch. We all see and feel differently about nature. When you sketch outside, never throw bad ones away. They will always tell you something, even if it's how not to do it again.

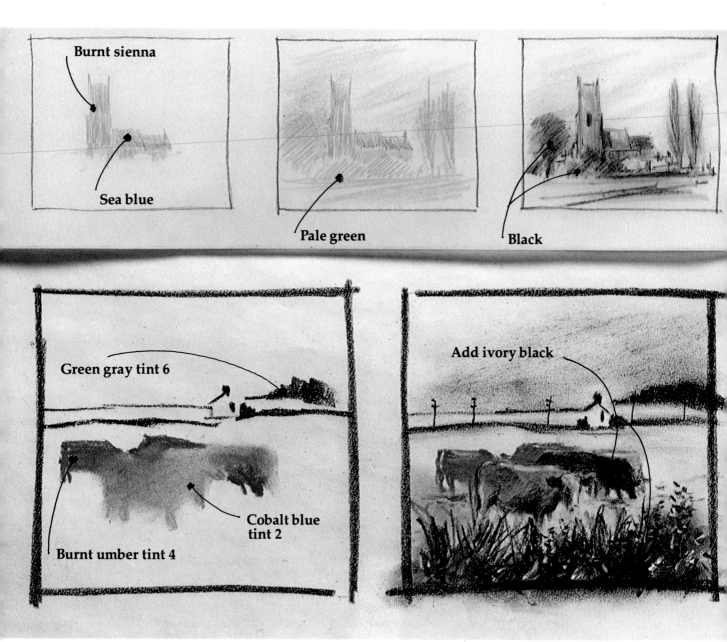

Ultramarine blue, alizarin crimson and yellow ochre

Yellow ochre and alizarin crimson

Fountain pen lines

Yellow ochre and ultramarine blue

Yellow ochre and alizarin crimson

Cerulean blue and alizarin crimson

Add yellow ochre

Yellow ochre, cerulean blue and alizarin crimson

Ultramarine blue, alizarin crimson and yellow ochre

Same colors as sky

How To Measure

Here's how to hold your pencil for measuring vertically (top) or horizontally (bottom).

I consider the starting of a sketch to be the most important part of the process. For this section, I'm assuming that you've chosen the materials, found your spot, settled down with the subject in front of you and are ready to sketch.

First decide what type of sketch you are going to do. This can save a lot of time and frustration. If you were to sketch your own chair, you would be very familiar with it and would understand everything you see because you know it. Look at your chosen subject and try to achieve the same sense of familiarity. If there are areas that you can't understand, or you can't see properly, move around to different viewpoints until you are familiar with what you are about to draw. This could take up to 15 minutes, depending on how complicated the subject is, but that time used correctly is a most important part of your sketch.

At this point you might understand everything you see, but how do you work out the relative sizes and positions of objects in your scene. Then how do you transpose them accurately on your paper? This section shows you how. Although you may find that *measuring* is tedious, or a bit mechanical, you must learn it. It is a very important skill. It is as much a part of sketching as putting pencil to paper.

You have no doubt seen an artist do it by holding an arm out with thumb up while looking at the subject. Rather than use a thumb, I prefer to use a pencil. Here's how: Hold your pencil at arm's length, vertically for vertical measuring and horizontally for horizontal measuring. Put your thumb along the near edge as your measuring *marker,* as shown above. Always keep your arm at the same distance from your eye during measuring. Otherwise, the comparative distances will not be consistent. Using arm's length avoids the problem. The object of the exercise is to measure the subject and apply the measurement to your paper proportionately.

Follow the exercise on the opposite page to get a good understanding of the process. Draw a part of your sketch, say house 3 on the paper (A). Now you want to get houses 1 to 7 on your sketch proportionately, as they appear in reality. Hold up your pencil to measure house 3. This becomes the *key measure.* As you move your hand along, see how many times the pencil goes into the length of the seven houses.

Let's say that it goes into it nine times. Check your original sketch (A) and using your pencil on the paper as a ruler, see whether the length of the house you have drawn will go along your paper nine times. With the starting sketch (A), it goes only about five times.

The solution is to draw a smaller house in the same sketch (B). By simple trial and error you will come to the size of the house that will be in proportion to the rest of your picture.

Then holding up the pencil to the real houses, measure how many times house 3 goes into houses 1 and 2. Suppose that you find that they are the same width. Therefore, on your sketchbook, you can measure from left to right, three houses, the third being house 3 (C).

Looking at your subject again, measure house 3 into house 4. Suppose it goes in twice. On your sketch, using your pencil as a ruler and your thumb as a marker, measure a distance twice as long as house 3 to the right of it. This gives the correct size for house 4 in the sketch. Continue in this way until you have sketched the row of houses from 1 to 7 (D). They should fit well on the paper.

Now to check the height of the houses, measure the width of house 3 by holding your pencil horizontally. With your thumb still in position, see how many times the width of the house goes into the height. Let's say that it fits exactly once, up to the bottom of the roof. Therefore, on your sketch, use the width of house 3 as the height of house 3 to the bottom of the roof (E). Then continue the process to determine the height of the roofs.

If you take time to do this, you can put as much detail and work into the houses as you want, knowing that your drawing will fit on the paper and be proportionately correct. Objects will be in the right relationship to each other.

The photo at right illustrates a real-life example. My first key measure would be the stern of the boat at right. That length goes across the picture approximately six times. Working this out would mean making sure that everything in my picture fits the paper proportionately.

Other main features that are the same size as the key measure are illustrated too. Notice that I found a half-size key measure. This helps for other measurements. Put the important subjects into position by measuring. As you draw the rest, they should fit into place correctly.

When you are measuring, don't be too rigid. If an area of the subject measures a key measure and a bit, then draw it on your sketch the size of a key measure and a bit. Some approximation is part of the process.

If I were to show you how to do this in person, it would take only five minutes. But explaining it this way may make it seem complicated to you. If you are still confused, read it again until you understand the method. Then practice with simple subjects. Frequent practice will train your eye to see the size of objects in relation to each other and then place them correctly on the paper.

When measuring, choose a key measure. In this case it is the width of the boat at right.

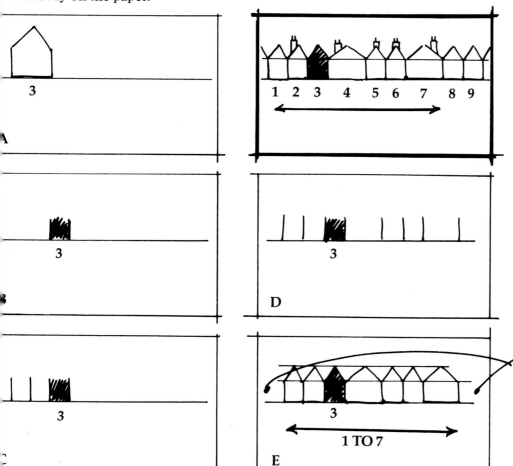

In drawing E, some space is left on both sides of the row for adding more information if necessary.

A Step-By-Step Sketch

Now that you know how to start a sketch, let's develop a simple sketch from start to finish to see how it works. At this stage you have chosen and observed your subject. You are sitting or standing comfortably. You know the type of sketch you are going to do. You know how to measure. And, finally, you have decided what your center of interest is.

Look at the last drawing of the illustrations at right. It is the completed sketch. Familiarizing yourself with the picture now will help you follow the process. All were done with a fountain pen on bristol board.

The first step is to draw the line of the main field. When you position this near the center of the page, you can add more foreground or sky later. I wanted this picture to be long and thin, because the long line of the farm buildings inspired me to draw this sketch.

The second step is to position the center of interest—in this case the buildings. Draw them in the third step.

In the fourth step, complete the buildings, emphasizing the lower part so they don't appear to float off the hill. Also draw in the new field.

In step five, put in the background hills. Draw the tree in step six. Now if you look at my sketch, I have drawn two more lines across, one above the buildings, and one below. This gives the long shape of the picture dominated by buildings.

Add more information if you have the time, as I did in step seven. Step eight shows the paths extended, with the gate and fence drawn in. These compositional elements "lead" you to the center of interest.

The completed sketch has a few more elements than step eight. The main difference is that the bold horizontal line indicates a different picture shape. If the sketch is cut off just above the tree, the sky is de-emphasized. This is the third composition possible with just this one simple sketch.

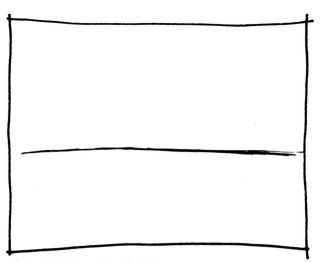

1) Establish line of main field.

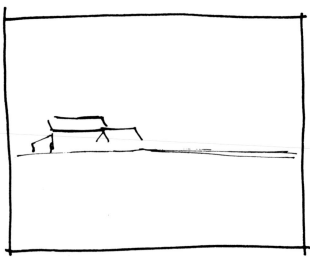

2) Locate center of interest.

3) Draw center of interest.

4) Finish buildings. Emphasize bottoms. Draw field.

7) Add more information—path and field.

5) Draw background hills.

8) Draw gate and extend path.

6) Finish tree. Two other lines determine a finished sketch.

9) Add details to finish sketch. New line makes a different composition.

Finishing A Sketch

Stop working on a sketch when you feel as if you have drawn long enough. This could be due to fatigue, hunger, cold, boredom or any number of other reasons. But the simple fact remains: You are sketching to enjoy yourself. When the enjoyment is finished, you are finished. Start another sketch or end the session.

On one occasion I had been sketching for most of the day by a wharf. I was tired, a bit chilly and ready to go home when I saw a group of boats that caught my eye. I thought they were a perfect group and decided to do a "quick" sketch—the last one before going home.

Well, the result was disastrous. You can see it on the opposite page, at upper left. I still can't make sense of it even now. It went wrong because I had tried to work too fast. There is nothing wrong with that, but I was tired and didn't *observe.* I drew it without "seeing." Unless you observe carefully every time, lines become meaningless.

As a basic rule, you should also consider stopping when you have the information on paper that you were after. That's what I did for the watercolor sketches on this page. The top two were done on 140-pound, cold-pressed watercolor paper, 20x15 inches. The one at bottom is from a 16x12-inch sketchbook. It was done very freely but I still have enough information to work from. I consider the bottom one a *pure* sketch. The other two were turned from sketches into paintings.

In the pencil sketch on the opposite page, upper right, I represented distance well, but made the middle distance and foreground confusing. This is because I used shading over the drawing. I should have stopped work on that sketch before I shaded the foreground.

The middle sketch in page 43 is open-pencil work. I think it fine because I left the wintery trees unfinished so I could get information on the sketch as to what was going on behind them. In addition, I made color notes on the sketch to make it easy to work from while painting a picture of it in the studio.

At bottom is a normal information sketch, which usually has line work and tonal shading. On this one I didn't do a color code so you could see the sketch better.

I included these examples to show that not every sketch is a great one! For one of them I didn't do enough work. In another I put too much work, the shading. And with the other two pencil sketches I was very happy.

FROM BERRY OAK PARK. 1982

SOMERTON 21 JAN 82

43

Questions And Answers

To get some specific points across, I decided to show three of my sketches to a group of artists and students so they could question me about them. Some of their questions and my answers make up other parts of this book. Here are some particularly useful ones:

Where did you start the bottom sketch?

I first positioned the tower of Windsor Castle in about the middle of the paper and worked out its size by measuring. This assured me that I could fit enough of the castle on the page. Then I positioned the river.

Why did you put the tower in the middle of the picture?

Because the tower and the flag are tallest, they tend to give the whole castle a triangular shape, making the castle look solid on the ground. To enhance the symmetry of the triangle, I put the tower in the center. Although it is the center of interest, I broke a rule and put it in the center of the sketch. Even so, the composition works well.

What could have inspired you to make the middle sketch?

I was out sketching during a severe winter, and as I walked up the road, I saw the machine. It was there to repair part of the ruined road. Because I had never seen anything like it before, I found it interesting. The result is a typical enjoyment sketch.

Where did you start it?

I positioned the machine first but made sure I had enough room for the break in the road. To my mind, it provides the drama, or atmosphere, of the sketch.

How do you scale a sketch to get the correct proportion of paper for a larger picture at home?

The illustration on this page shows you how. Align the lower-right corner of a sketch with the lower-right corner of the fresh paper. Use a ruler, or a straight edge of some kind, to continue the diagonal of the sketch onto the fresh paper. Wherever you draw a line parallel with the top of the sketch to meet your diagonal line, drop a perpendicular line down, parallel to the side of the page. That area will be exactly proportional to your sketch. It is an elegantly simple way to make your finished work either larger or smaller than the finished sketch.

What inspired you to sketch the landscape at top?

I was not so much inspired as commissioned. It is a view of a part of Wales in the spring. I had four glorious days sketching in the area and eventually worked on four large 36x24-inch canvases. It was a fabulous assignment that both I and the client enjoyed. On this sketch I worked on heavy, smooth paper, using pencil first, then watercolors, then felt pen.

Where did you start?

I established the hills farthest away first. Then I worked on the distinct hillside of trees running down from the center to the right side of the picture.

Is the hillside covered in trees, or not?

That is a reasonable question because from the sketch it is difficult to know exactly what the dark area is. In fact it is covered with trees, but because it is a sketch and I *knew* they were trees, representing them very accurately did not matter.

Why is sketching important to you?

It teaches me to observe. Also, it takes me outdoors to be inspired enough by nature to record it. I consider it the life blood of my inspiration. If you can go out sketching, then you must.

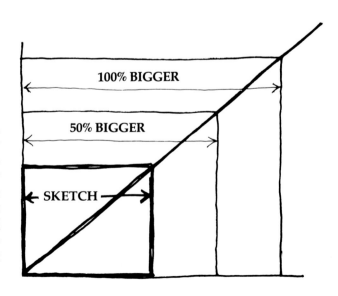

Sketching Movement

When you are learning to sketch, you should stick with stationary objects. You'll have enough things to worry about without trying to reproduce motion.

But now let's assume that you want to try sketching a moving subject. The initial preparations are identical to those for stationary subjects. Choose the subject; stand or sit comfortably; and decide the type of information you are looking for. The next stage is to observe and understand your subject. This is most important for capturing movement. Measuring is important, but it can be very difficult, if not impossible.

I have tried to come up with a sure-fire formula that you can use when sketching a moving subject. Unfortunately, I don't have one! Nevertheless, there are certain ways to deal with a moving subject that will help you master sketching it. When you have spent five minutes drawing a horse and it casually walks away before you have finished working on its hind quarters, you can get frustrated.

The most important assets are practice and self-control. These are followed by observation and understanding of the subject. For example, let's go back to horses. First, you must look at them and study their most outstanding features. You will find they can stand still for minutes at a time. Look for the obvious key positions of their anatomy. Where does a foreleg start, and how long is it compared to the depth of the body, and so on. This way you are measuring and positioning through observation, before you start to draw.

Such observation could last 20 to 30 minutes, or longer if you are enjoying yourself. It's up to you, but don't "draw" with your eyes for too long. Otherwise, it will be more difficult to start sketching. When you do begin to sketch, don't rush and go faster than you are capable of. Sketch at your own speed, observing carefully. If your subject moves, stop and start with another. You may find that the subject regains its original position or that another horse takes up the same pose.

Never worry about finishing one horse completely. The true learning comes from the observing. The sketching merely records what you see. This combination of activities will quickly give you a good understanding of your subject.

Naturally, the more you do the more your sketches will flow, particularly as you understand more about your subject. If I were to sketch horses for two hours, I would start by spending 30 minutes wandering around looking and observing, absorbing the atmosphere. Then I would sketch for the next 20 minutes. Chances are it would not be very good, but I would be loosening up, relaxing and getting the "feel" of the subject.

For the next hour I would work very hard, concentrating intently on the subjects and sketching them as well as I could. It is from this time that the real information would come. If my sketches worked, I'd be pleased. Then my concentration would start to lapse. The results of the last 10 minutes would resemble those of the first 20 minutes.

If the horses are walking, observe them, and then draw. You will notice the movement and the shapes that keep recurring as they move. Drawn lines will be dictated by what you have observed. This sounds easy, but if you don't practice it will be very difficult. This applies to virtually any moving subject.

One way of training your eye to retain an image long enough to draw its shape reasonably well is to sketch movement on your TV screen. Though difficult, it's possible. You won't finish anything, and your sketchbook may seem to be filled with unsatisfactory work, but these sketches are simply a means to an end. They are a way of training your brain to *work and observe* faster than normal. You will learn to look for and see things that hadn't occurred to you before. You will practice seeing in seconds how to simplify shape and form.

When sketching movement, remember my rules: be patient, observe, look for simple shapes and form, work at your own speed, and practice, practice, practice! If you aren't successful in sketching movement, don't worry. Stick to the vast range of stationary subjects—so long as you enjoy it!

As shown at right, people on the beach are interesting subjects to sketch. The best part is that you can do it in warmth and comfort! These sketches also show you the type of detail I prefer when sketching moving subjects. All were done at different times and in different places.

18 MARCH 79 · SHACKLEFORD   A3 GUILDFORD.

BOURNEMOUTH
BEACH
AUG. 76.

31 JAN 82 OTTERTON MILL

First stage.

Second stage.

Third stage.

Pencil Exercise I

On the following pages, I have taken six subjects and worked each one through its progressive stages for you to follow and copy, using different media. You'll notice that I have sketched these in my own style. It's not important if your style and method differ a bit. At this stage of your sketching it helps to have some guidance in a certain direction. This way you can determine whether it suits you or not. If it does, fine. If not, then through experience you can deviate from a workable method and style to find your own.

For all of these exercises, I made finished sketches outside. Then at home I resketched them, stopping at different stages so they could be photographed. However, the progression you see is actual. They are on the same sketch.

FIRST STAGE

Establish the distant, main field by drawing a line across the paper with a 3B pencil. Put in the line of the hills in the distance and then draw the river. Add the rear field line, the path, willow trees on the left bank, and the dark tree in the middle distance to the right of the willow. Throughout the first and second stages, hold your pencil in the long position.

SECOND STAGE

Shade in the distant hills and work from left to right on the trees in the middle distance. Start with the dark tree on the right side of the willows. When you come to the willow on the right side of the river bank, draw in its shape. Let your pencil float around, applying different pressures. Form and shape the trees by shading freely. Don't try to copy mine exactly.

THIRD STAGE

Still working with the pencil in the long position, shade the willows in the direction of leaf and branch growth. Work from the bottom up. Keep the shading light where the dark, middle-distance tree shows against the willow.

Darken the trunks with your pencil held in the short position and add the shadow underneath. Now work very lightly to suggest the trees left of the willow. With your pencil held in the long position again, draw in the willow on the right side of

Finished sketch, 16-1/2x11-1/2 inches.

the river and the cows in the middle distant field.

Of course, cows move around. So normally I put in the cows wherever they fit well in the sketch, not necessarily at this third stage.

LAST STAGE

At this stage put in any detail you want to give form to certain areas. For instance, draw in some grass on the left bank coming down to the river. Or darken the far bank where the river bends to the left. Most of this work can be done with the pencil held in the short position.

Now draw in the gate, fence and signpost. Shade in the reflections in the river with downward strokes and then draw your pencil across the river to give the impression of movement.

Now add grass detail to darken the edge of the river and the path. Finally, add the couple of cows that have wandered into the field left of the willows. Shade in the clouds.

First stage.

Second stage.

Third stage.

Pencil Exercise II

I didn't have to go far to sketch this scene—it is a street in my town. It's proof that you don't need exotic, spectacular scenes to sketch. Worthy subjects are all around you.

The first stage is done with a pencil in the short position. It gives complete pencil control for careful detail work. The long position offers less control. The flat position has least of all, but it gives the greatest freedom of movement and covering power.

I didn't draw in the eye level when I worked the sketch, but I did locate it. I referred to it to check anything that looked wrong as I was drawing.

FIRST STAGE

Using a 2B pencil, establish the right side of the prominent building on the left side of the street. Use one straight line. Then draw in the rest of the building to get the correct proportions. If you were on location, you would measure as described on page 38. Carefully draw the shapes starting at the chimneys and work down toward the windows.

Make the right side of the building dark as you come to it. This will "anchor" your sketch as you continue drawing. Now position the line of houses and trees in the background. Put in the road and houses on the right side of the street at the end.

Finally, draw in the front car and work back, fixing the position of the other cars. You might find when doing the first stage that you also establish other parts of the sketch. As you draw in one part, it automatically gives you a reference point for another section of the drawing. This is what happens when you are working outside and building up a sketch.

SECOND STAGE

With your pencil in the long position, shade in the background houses and trees. Draw the railings over the bridge and the streetlights on the left. Draw all of this, keeping the tones light to keep the distance in its proper place. Finally, put in the gutters and window of the building on the right side. Make it dark because this helps establish the tonal values of the background. Draw the bridge railings and streetlights with your pencil in the short position.

THIRD STAGE

Now the sketch is well-established on paper. Add detail to the large building at left. Hold your pencil in the short position. Divide the windows with faint

Finished sketch, 11-1/2x8 inches.

pencil lines, then shade in the dark window panes individually. Don't try to make the shading an exact shape. Otherwise, it will lose some of its character. See what I mean by looking at the closeup illustration at the bottom of the page.

Shade the chimneys, roof and walls with the pencil held in the short position. The pencil must have a chisel-shaped point to give a broad stroke. Also shade in the wall in front of the inn and put an edge to the road going off to the left.

LAST STAGE

Now draw in the three objects in front of the wall. One is the menu board, another the utility box, and the third an ornamental feature. Next draw the cars with your pencil in the short position. Add a few more details to the buildings on the right. Because they are very foreshortened, they appear simply as dark and light shapes. Put in the television antennaes and sketch in the shadows across the road, holding your pencil in the long position.

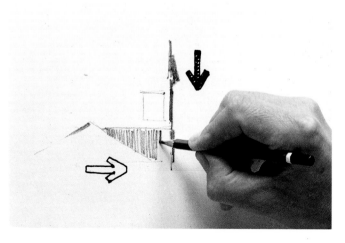

Charcoal Exercise

First stage.

Second stage.

Third stage.

As I work with charcoal more, I have come to like it more. But I prefer to limit its use to landscapes because in my experience that is what it works best with. It makes nature seem undefined, and yet complete.

This exercise is very simple and took only about 30 minutes to sketch, but I think that it shows the beauty of charcoal drawing. I used a charcoal stick about two inches long. I held it in short and flat positions. The long position could break a stick.

In the charcoal sketching set described earlier, I didn't illustrate a fixative spray because the attraction of charcoal is the simplicity of the equipment. I keep a can in the car, so that when I have finished sketching, I can spray my sketches before going home.

FIRST STAGE

Establish the line of the hill, the road and then the background trees. Start the trees from the bottom upward, drawing the branches in the direction in which they grow.

SECOND STAGE

Now draw in the large foreground tree by scrubbing the stick up and down the trunk to get the density you want. You will find that the grain of some rough papers helps to give texture to tree bark. Work the branches outward in the direction of growth, then put shading to the right of the tree to imply shadow.

THIRD STAGE

This stage introduces smudging—one of the delights of charcoal. It enables you to add tone to large areas. By working on the area and adding more charcoal, you can build up the tonal work to put plenty of depth into your sketch.

For the smaller trees, use your index finger to smudge the background trees together and in places, over the foreground tree. If you find that the tone needs to be darker, add more charcoal over the trees and smudge it in.

LAST STAGE

Draw the background trees again, finely, over the original ones. Try dragging the stick across the paper to get a slightly different branch effect. Then draw in the main tree and add more branches, working some over the smudged area. As you do this, you will see how the smudged area recedes. The main tree seems to come forward. Add the shadows across the road, put in some accents on the road edge and, finally, draw the fence.

Finished sketch, 7x9 inches.

Pen Exercise

This sketch was executed near the spot where I made the sketch shown on page 7. I enjoyed sketching the area for eventual paintings, so I have sketched it quite a few times in many different moods.

Variety is one of the great advantages of a lakeside or seaside area. The scene is constantly changing with the seasons and weather. And boats and people offer plenty of activity. It should be a natural place for any artist.

I did the sketch on location directly with a fountain pen on bristol board, but for this exercise I drew it in first with a 2B pencil. This was a guide because I was working from a sketch, not the real thing. I worked on smooth bristol board.

FIRST STAGE

In this exercise, start from the center of interest. Locate the water level on your paper and draw it in with your pen. You can draw the main parts of the sketch with your pencil first, but if you feel confident, try using a fountain pen directly.

Next, draw in the top of the wharf and the boathouse. Shade it in downstrokes with the pen. Then draw in the boats in front of the boathouse.

SECOND STAGE

Draw in the hills in the background and the water line to the right of the boathouse. Add the houses to the left and then the cars. Working to the right of the boathouse, create an impression of an untidy group of boats by letting your pen move freely. Draw in the masts, making sure that you draw these in at different angles—some straight, some leaning. See the detail of the sketch at the bottom of page 55.

THIRD STAGE

Now draw in the rocks at the edge of the water. Start at the top-left side and work down to the bottom right. Shade in the rocks as you work, keeping most of them dark against the water. As you work down, put in the three people when you come to them.

LAST STAGE

Draw in the wharf details—telephone poles, yacht masts, people and little boats. Now shade in the distant hills and draw in the foreground boat.

First stage.

Second stage.

Third stage.

Finished sketch, 7x9 inches.

Treat the reflections very freely, working the pen in horizontal strokes, backward and forward. For the boathouse reflections, masts and telegraph pole, draw the pen line vertically. Start at the top and work in a free wiggly stroke downward. Add a few horizontal strokes to the left of the boathouse to give the impression of water movement. Finally, put a little more detail into the beach and rocks.

Watercolor Exercise

First stage.

Second stage.

Third stage.

It was late afternoon with the sun going down over the hills when I was inspired to make this quick watercolor sketch. The misty light seemed to merge shapes and create mysterious silhouettes. I decided that the most attractive silhouette would be the tree against the church. I used 140-pound, cold-pressed watercolor paper.

FIRST STAGE

First draw the picture with an HB pencil. Then wet the sky area down to the roofs with clean water, using a No. 10 sable brush. Mix a wash of ultramarine blue and alizarin crimson. Work this into the sky first and, as you work down, add a little yellow ochre. Add cadmium yellow pale and work over the hill and down to the roof tops to get the effect of late afternoon light.

SECOND STAGE

When the sky is dry, use the same No. 10 brush and a mix of the same colors to paint in the distant fields on the right side and the houses just below.

Still using the same colors, only stronger—by mixing more pigment and less water—paint in the church steeple. Start at the top and work down. Change your mix of colors as you paint to give the sketch some realism.

Then work left and right of the steeple, painting in the houses. Don't paint over the windows. Leave the paper showing through. While this is still wet, mix some Hooker's green No. 1 with your color and paint in the grass in front of the church. Allow it to touch the wet paint and run in places.

THIRD STAGE

Now with your size No. 6 sable brush, mix ultramarine blue, alizarin crimson and yellow ochre. Use the mix to paint in the wall. Leave white areas showing through and try to paint the wall stone by stone. A lot of them run into each other, but this will give the effect of a stone wall.

Mix Hooker's green No. 1 with your color and paint in the grass lawn. With a little yellow ochre and alizarin crimson, paint the road.

Mix ultramarine blue, alizarin crimson, yellow ochre and Hooker's green No. 1 to make a strong dark tone. Use it to paint the tree at the back. Work from the bottom and, keeping the paint wet, sketch in the trunk out to the branches. While the paint is

Finished sketch, 14-1/2x10-1/2 inches.

still wet, drag a dry brush back into the branches to give the feathery effect of small branches. See the detail below.

While this area is still wet, paint in some small branches with a No. 2 sable brush. When the whole tree is nearly dry, start the main, foreground tree. Use the same paint mix but darken it a bit more. Repeat the process and work over the rear tree.

LAST STAGE

Mix Hooker's green No. 1, yellow ochre, alizarin crimson and a touch of ultramarine blue. With a No. 6 sable brush, paint in the foreground field, leaving the fence area as white paper.

Next paint in the windows, using a mix of yellow, red and blue. Paint little blobs to suggest windowpanes. Put more work into the wall, by drawing some stones with your brush, using the same color as for the windowpanes.

Now work on the foreground tree again, making it darker. Put in more small branches. Using dark color, put shadows on the white fence and signpost. Add accent colors where you need definition. Finally, using ultramarine blue, alizarin crimson and yellow ochre, paint in the shadow of the tree.

First stage.

Second stage.

Third stage.

Pastel Exercise

When you are out sketching a rural scene like this one, details are easy to overlook. If the sun is out and the area is bathed in bright, midday light, the scene can look flat and uninteresting. If it is a dull, overcast day, you could miss details in the building because it could merge into the gray background. Therefore, the best time to view and sketch a scene of this kind is when there is sun around with clouds casting large shadows. This will add drama to the scene.

I used Ingres 100% rag paper for this pastel exercise. The paper comes in different shades.

FIRST STAGE

Draw in the main features with a 2B pencil. If you were outside and working quickly, you might find that you could start with pastel, without doing any pencil drawing. Now, using the long side of a yellow ochre tint 2, sketch the sky area in broad strokes from left to right. In the same way sketch cobalt blue tint 2 over the top, leaving the area by the road clear. Smudge the colors together with your finger.

Now with gray green tint 6, paint in the distant hills and draw in the hedges of the fields and road.

SECOND STAGE

Work burnt umber tint 4 onto the distant hills and rub it in a bit with your finger. Now work in the fields down to the farm, using first a little yellow ochre tint 2 and then green tint 3 on the distant fields, painting it stronger down toward the farm. Rub in the colors to tone down the area. Next paint in the farm roofs with purple gray tint 4, and work over the shadow side with green gray tint 6. The shadow side is at right because the sun is on the left.

THIRD STAGE

Paint in the sunlit walls of the buildings with yellow ochre tint 2, and use green gray tint 6 to paint in the dark wall in front of the buildings. With the same pastel colors, paint in features of the farm—such as chimneys, windows, doors, and the trees on the left side. Smudge in the trees with your finger.

Finished sketch, 14-1/2x10-1/2 inches.

Paint in the foreground field, using lizard green tint 3 up to the shadow area. Then work in some burnt umber tint 4 up to the farm wall and into the green field. Smudge some green gray tint 6 into the farm building here and there, and into the field on the left. Now with burnt umber tint 4, paint in the field behind the farm on the right side. With green gray tint 6, paint in the hedges. Smudge some of the color across the field. Finally, put the telegraph poles in the background.

LAST STAGE

Using yellow ochre tint 2, paint in the road, from distance to foreground. Then smudge it in to tone it down. Now with green gray tint 6, paint in the shadow on the foreground field. Next paint in the shapes of the buildings, telephone poles and trees in the foreground with ivory black. Add a little to the shadow area of the field. Use the black in various places on the farm buildings to add distinct shape. Finally, paint over the road where the sun is shining with yellow ochre tint 2.

Using Sketches At Home

One of the rewards of having drawn sketches outside is that you can use them later to work on larger paintings at home. A full sketchbook represents lots of good information and inspiration when you don't want to go outside to sketch. At these times it is probably best to paint some of them at home.

When searching through my sketchbooks for sketches to reproduce in this book, I was able to relive many happy moments just by looking at them. There were sketches that I had never redone, and some were almost 10 years old! After so much time had gone by I was able to see them in a different context and wanted to paint from them right away.

I love to come across an old sketch and paint from it in watercolor. It gives me an opportunity to try different techniques and to illustrate nature's and my changing moods. One advantage in working from the same sketch numerous times is that you get to know the subjects so well that you can concentrate more on the painting, rather than drawing.

Here is the original sketch described above. It was the inspiration for the three watercolors on the next page.

TIPTON ST JOHNS 31 MAY 81 - FLOODS.

For these reasons a full sketchbook is a definite artistic asset. You should always sketch when you have the opportunity. It is too easy to be lazy and put off doing a sketch. When I go somewhere and see something that inspires me, I have to fight against putting it off until later. In my experience, it is bad policy to postpone doing it. When you see the subject later, it may look completely different due to the light or weather. It may be no longer worth sketching. Also you may not even see the subject again!

There is only one way to fill your sketchbook—keep one with you all the time and use it often. When you see something that inspires you, sketch it. But believe me, it is not as easy as it sounds. Even a professional artist can have difficulties. You can't always stop just when you want to. But if you make an effort, you will soon see your sketchbook pages gradually fill with valuable information. The following examples show what I mean.

I did the sketch at left about a year ago during a rainy season when many fields were flooded. Although I had never worked from it before, I decided to paint it in watercolor. The finished paintings at right show that with just one sketch you can illustrate three different moods. All three were painted on the same type of paper—about 11x9 inch, 140-pound, cold-pressed watercolor paper.

The top painting is rendered as I remembered the original scene. I kept the painting simple, to create the feeling of freshness you get after a rainfall. Notice how the water is painted very simply, with the foreground left as white paper.

For the middle painting, I *imagined* that it was early morning and the scene was a bit foggy. I achieved this by wetting the paper and running the first wash over the whole area, leaving only one or two areas of paper white to represent the water. The house is paper white too. When the paper was dry, I added a second wash of color and then worked the dark area under the trees.

The bottom painting is a snow scene. I painted the sky dark with Payne's gray, yellow ochre and alizarin crimson. Using the same colors, I "drew" the picture with a No. 6 sable brush. The secret of this effect is in what you *don't* paint. I left plenty of white paper showing through to represent snow.

Making A Specific Sketch

I decided to write an account of this day's sketching because it embodies all of the problems of making a specific sketch, particularly the need for careful planning. At the beginning of this book I explained what a specific sketch was and described some of the problems you might have. But if you are ever in a situation demanding that you get it right the first time—such as a special event or weather condition—this section will help.

I had been asked by the BBC if they could film me on location painting a watercolor for later television broadcast. Naturally I was thrilled and excited to be asked, but then I became a bit nervous when it dawned on me what I had agreed to do. It would entail working outside at the mercy of the elements; painting a scene in watercolor that the camera could also see; and describing what I am doing as I paint. It was going to be a totally new experience for me!

I met the director of the film at my studio to discuss the details and, from the moment he arrived, he put me at ease. My anxieties faded away. The plans were simple. I was to work by a local river for a certain day. Then it was up to me to work out *my* plans.

I decided to go down to the river the day before filming and find a suitable spot. But there were certain restrictions. It had to be near a parking lot because filming equipment had to be carried along the river bank. The scene had to include the river, and the subject had to be simple. This way viewers could see it clearly and I would be able to describe what I

That's me on the right sketching the scene during filming.

was painting. I also had to be in a position that would allow the camera to shoot from behind me. When I looked around, I found plenty of perfect scenes, but for most of them the camera would have had to have been in the river! Even so, I found a good spot and an alternate after about an hour of searching.

This planning day was to be a trial run. I used 22x15-1/2-inch, cold-pressed watercolor paper, so I brought four sheets on a board. I also took a small fold-up table to support the paints. Normally, I don't take a table, but it was the only way for the camera to see me mixing colors. In addition, I had a small chair, pencils, paintbox, brushes, eraser, water and a container, and a knife for resharpening pencils. I always carry bandages in my bag, in case of cuts. It may seem overcautious, but if you cut your finger, it can make painting messy.

The only factor I couldn't control was the weather, but the morning of the rehearsal was superb. The sun was in a clear blue sky and it was warm. After a relaxing picnic lunch, I set up and started to paint.

After an hour's painting, it dawned on me that the subject was not right for my purposes. Reluctantly, I stopped, feeling very annoyed with myself. I packed up and moved my equipment to the alternate spot, shown at left. I set up again and started a new painting.

After about half an hour, I knew that it was right. Why I considered it my second choice I'll never know, but it was lucky I had planned for it in

This is a photograph of the scene I painted for the BBC.

Here's the finished watercolor sketch, 22x15-1/2 inches.

advance. Otherwise, the film would have covered the first, and less desirable, spot.

While painting, I worked out in my mind how to break up the various steps for the viewers—where to stop and start and describe for the camera the following day. I finished the painting and was pleased with it. I then marked the spot with a pile of stones.

The following morning my only worries were the weather and local cows. I didn't want them in view. Luckily, all went well. Both the weather and the cows cooperated. The day was set. The director arrived, and we went down to the village to meet the cameraman and sound engineer.

We all carried our respective equipment down the river bank. It was such a beautiful day that it felt as though we were all going for a picnic down by the river. When we reached my stone marker, I set up my equipment.

Because I had already been through the experience, I felt at home, but not quite relaxed. Once everybody was ready and it was explained how I was to start, I got over my first faltering sentences and did well. The finished sketch is shown above.

We went through the whole day without a hitch. I am sure that my planning was the key, in addition to the professionalism of the crew. It was a happy day, as sketching should be.

A week later when the film was edited, we saw the program and for the first time in my life, I could actually see myself working. There were fabulous close-ups showing the brush mixing colors on the palette and putting washes over the paper. After I had watched the film, I felt relaxed for the first time since the initial telephone call.

Points To Remember

Put his head in car!

FUNNY NEW FOREST DONKEY!

9 Cw

- Buy the best equipment you can afford.
- Carry a small pencil sketching set with you and use it whenever possible.
- When something inspires you, sketch it.
- Be warm and comfortable when sketching.
- Start with simple subjects.
- Observe your subject carefully before sketching.
- Practice using your pencil.
- Never throw away your sketches.
- Don't put notes on a watercolor sketch.
- Put color notes on your black-and-white sketches.
- Enjoy your sketching—it should be fun!